S0-ARP-710

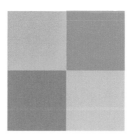

| | |
|---:|:---|
| Editor | Andrea Swank |
| Art Direction | Sandi Salyer and Ed Gregory |
| Creative Director | Lisa Eisenberg |
| Chief Creative Officer | Bob Tulini |
| Photography | Shawn-Erik Toth |
| Cartoonist | Jeanine Hattas |
| Illustration | Sandi Salyer |

Copyright © 2012 Shawn K. Smith, Ann M. Chavez, and Garret W. Seaman. All rights reserved worldwide.

Published by Modern Teacher Press

This publication is protected under the U.S. Copyright Act of 1976 and all other applicable international, federal, state and local laws, and all rights are reserved, including resale rights: no part of this document or the related matter may be reproduced or transmitted in any form, by any means (electronic, photocopying, recording, or otherwise) without the written permission of the author. Contact modernteacherpress.com for more information.

This book identifies product names and services known to be trademarks, registered trademarks, or service marks of their respective holders. They are used throughout this book in an editorial fashion only. In addition, terms suspected of being trademarks, registered trademarks, or service marks have been appropriately capitalized, although Modern Teacher Press cannot attest to the accuracy of this information. Use of a term in this book should not be regarded as affecting the validity of any trademark, registered trademark, or service mark.

Note: We have tried to recreate events and conversations from our memories of our time spent in public education in order to illustrate key concepts and principles from the book. In order to maintain people's anonymity and privacy we have changed the names of individuals and places. We have also changed some identifying characteristics and details such as physical properties and locations.

Although the authors and publisher have made every effort to ensure that the information in this book was correct at press time, the authors and publisher do not assume and hereby disclaim any liability to any party for any loss, damage, or disruption caused by errors or omissions, whether such errors or omissions result from negligence, accident, or any other cause.

Library of Congress Control Number: 2012944240

ISBN: 9780983886211

# Teacher as Architect®

## Instructional design and delivery for the modern teacher

SHAWN K. **SMITH**

ANN M. **CHAVEZ**

GARRETT W. **SEAMAN**

Dedication

*For today's teachers*

Make no little plans; they have no magic to stir men's blood …

Make big plans, aim high in hope and work.

Daniel H. Burnham
American Architect (1846—1912)

Contents

# Introduction:

# Core Principle 1: Designing with Purpose

# Core Principle 3: High-Impact Teaching Behaviors

# Core Principle 4: Managing Student Performance

# Appendix:

# Introduction

Teaching matters most.

It seems ordinary until you consider the scope of it: over the course of a day, week, month, and school year, you alone make thousands of decisions, both deliberate and instinctive, that affect how your students think, what they think about, and how well they achieve.

Put that way, it seems overwhelming.

So you must have wondered, as we did, what our most effective teachers do in their classrooms every day—how they think and execute, the decisions they make, the lessons they plan. How do they respond to students during these unprecedented times of change?

To answer these questions, we examined the lessons we learned in our own classrooms and those we've observed over the years. What we found was a noticeable pattern in how great teachers were going about their work.

Smith and Chavez have been school and district administrators for the last decade and have coached and supervised thousands of teachers and classrooms. We began questioning why some of our teachers were producing more than a year's worth of growth from their students while others were not. We combined our observations with student achievement data and the results challenged our assumptions of teacher practice—so as the last decade unfolded, we began to formally observe, describe, and document the discernible differences between good classrooms and great classrooms.

What we found could fill a book. So we wrote it.

Over the course of our 20+ years in public education, we deliberately captured great teachers' specific decisions and behaviors. We have organized these behaviors around a set of four core principles and created a powerful set of practical tools to improve instructional design and delivery. The book you have in your hands, *Teacher as Architect®,* will:

▶ Document and describe two decades of observations of the teachers who consistently deliver over a year's worth of academic growth for their students

▶ Link these observations to historic and contemporary research

▶ Organize the research and best practices into useable tools for teachers

▶ Include new ideas and trends emerging with digital media, web 2.0 and 3.0 tools

▶ Empower teachers to build their own plans from this information

▶ Provide a vehicle for teachers to experience this deeply personal work together

## Building a Classroom

The **four core principles** behind great teaching, the foundation of our book, connect the essential elements of **purposeful planning and design, customized learning for future skills,** the strength of **high-impact teaching** behaviors, and committed **management of student performance.** Then we identified the framework that gets at the heart of what we do: **we *design* instruction; we *build* according to standards; we *test* for validity; and we *create physical and virtual* places where students can thrive. We realized: *teachers are architects of learning.***

*Teacher as Architect* is written through the eyes of classroom teachers because that's who we are. We have seen, experienced, and believe in the power of teachers to build their own instructional plans in the context of larger school or district coherence. This book is about empowering you, the classroom teacher, to design a blueprint that meets your students' needs. This book, and your journey through it, is about building learning and classrooms, better.

While not a new initiative, *Teacher as Architect* is innovatively written as something you will experience and participate in. This book and its tools are intended to help teachers improve their craft. This book takes you on a journey, immersing you in practical hands-on tools to expand and refine the artistry and science of your teaching, asking you to reflect actively on your teaching experiences and the ideas you are reading. To help you on your way, the following chapter elements act as guide posts for your journey through the book.

A Teacher's Story begins each chapter and is a brief vignette or humorous piece reflecting our own experiences in education.

Connect and Reflect asks you to engage with the information in the chapter, drawing on your own teaching and experiences.

Why We Do What We Do is a synthesis of current educational trends and topics, research, and best practices that detail both our pedagogical inheritance and our current educational environment.

Guiding Questions frame the thinking and learning through the chapter.

Connecting to Classroom Practice features explanation and examples from the field that illustrate *Teacher as Architect* core principles and provides tools and process maps to aid you in constructing your own classroom.

Blueprint Essentials are a summary of key learnings from the chapter.

In the Library suggests follow-up readings and related resources.

Reflection and Action asks you to think about and journal your personal next steps.

Our guideposts will help a classroom teacher take this journey alone, but for a more meaningful experience, travel with a friend, companions, grade level teams, or across schools or districts. Our goal is that you and colleagues construct a shared meaning of the instructional and decision-making process so all students achieve success.

To help you on your path, we group and examine the TAA content into
Four Core Principles, and this creates the foundation of the book.

## Core Principle 1
### Designing with Purpose

Design a blueprint for classroom instruction
and strategically consider a range of choices
to motivate student success.

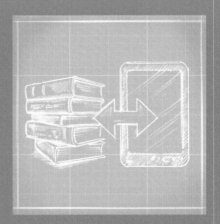

## Core Principle 2
### Customizing 21st Century Learning

Know the 21st century learner, leverage a range
of advanced technology tools that will provide
multiple learning pathways that customize and
enrich the learning experience.

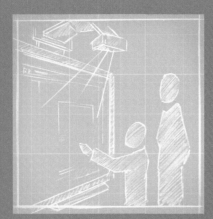

## Core Principle 3
### High-Impact Teaching Behaviors

Teach the blueprint by using
a series of high-impact behaviors
associated with student learning.

## Core Principle 4
### Managing Student Performance

From multiple sources, collect and analyze
evidence of student learning to understand
each student's mastery of specific content
and readiness for new content.

*Teacher as Architect* provides the plan and tools for you to organize all the things teachers do, think, and decide into a strategic classroom blueprint. While this book is about helping teachers connect the isolated parts of instructional design and delivery into a coherent whole, it is written to help you maximize your teaching effectiveness. It is our intention that you reach the end of the book, and your journey, in a different place than when you started.

This book is for the modern teacher. What does it mean to be a modern teacher? We believe the modern teacher understands our history and is grounded in our profession's research and best practices. As professionals, we understand the role we play in our larger society and how our public schools contribute to a strong America. We also believe the modern teacher understands teaching is both an art and science. We are continuously looking for ways to increase our effectiveness with the students we teach. With a strong grasp of our past, the modern teacher is also forward thinking. We take calculated risks that extend our impact with kids. We look for new and innovative ways to reach today's students. We understand the digital natives in our classrooms today and design and build learning accordingly. We are proud to be on this journey in public education. We are happy to be a part of your journey.

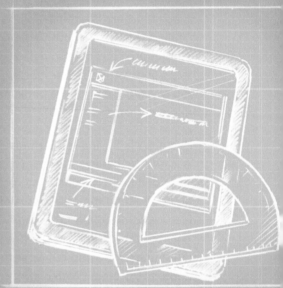

## Core Principle 1

# Designing
## with Purpose

Design a blueprint for
classroom instruction
and strategically consider
a range of choices to
motivate student success.

The chapters that support Core Principle 1, Designing with Purpose, are the foundation of the book. We walk you through how to design a blueprint for classroom instruction that strategically considers your range of choices to create student success. We start our discussion with three questions:

1. What do kids need to know and be able to do?

2. When do I teach these things?

3. How will I plan for them?

In Chapter 1 Society's Needs and the New Ask we clarify our mission by examining perspectives on American public schooling and education through an historical and contemporary cultural lens. We draw on contemporary voices, thinking critically about the differences between what children needed to know 100 or 200 years ago and what our children will need to know in 20 or 30 years. We conclude by building on our understanding of how humans think and what higher-order thinking means to educators.

Chapter 2 – Classifying Knowledge and Cognition: New Higher-Order Thinking in 21st Century Classrooms helps us understand critical thinking, knowledge, cognition, and how they interact with one another.

Chapter 3 – Understanding Common Core State Standards delves into the Common Core State Standards and how they relate to lesson planning and learning.

Chapter 4 – Are My Students Learning? The Power of Assessments begins by asking: *Are my students learning?* As the chapter unfolds, we demonstrate the role of assessment in building our classroom plan, and identify and define the many types of assessment options.

Chapter 5 – Brain Storm: Four Colliding Forces explores brain research, learning theory, pedagogy, and instructional strategies and how contemporary teachers connect the different perspectives.

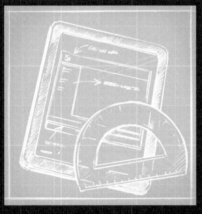

# Core Principle 1
## Designing with Purpose

Design a blueprint for classroom
instruction and strategically
consider a range of choices
to motivate student success.

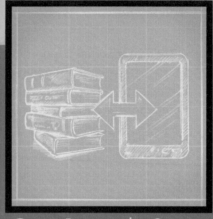

# Core Principle 2
## Customizing 21st Century Learning

Know the 21st century learner, leverage
a range of advanced technology tools
that will provide multiple learning
pathways that customize and enrich
the learning experience.

# Core Principle 3
## High-Impact Teaching Behaviors

Teach the blueprint by using
a series of high-impact behaviors
associated with student learning.

# Core Principle 4
## Managing Student Performance

From multiple sources, collect and
analyze evidence of student learning
to understand each student's mastery
of specific content and readiness for
new content.

# Designing with Purpose

Know your 21st Century Learner

Digital Learning Systems

21st Century Tools

Learning Pathways

Standards

Assessment

Curriculum Mapping & Unit Planning

Cognitive Growth Targets

Pedagogy & Lesson Design

© Modern Teacher Press 2012

# Chapter 1

# Society's Needs
## and the New
# Ask

## A Teacher's Story: First Classroom

*Miss Blake was walking down the hall with the principal, excitedly chatting about the school. She'd been assigned a 6th grade homeroom at a middle school in the city where she grew up, and her first real classroom awaited her at the end of the hall...excited, proud, and anxious they entered Room 6. There was a title on the board. It did not say student teacher or substitute teacher. It said, **Miss Blake, Teacher.** The room, **her** room, is filled with furniture and chairs piled high in the middle of the room, brick walls, a white board, a smart board, and a passcode to access the school's digital learning system...and instantly her mind starts to race, rearranging, organizing, designing the space for learning...so many possibilities and all hers to decide. The principal was talking but she didn't hear a thing. Understanding, the principal left her alone to get started.*

*Taking down a chair and sitting on the edge of a table, feet dangling, Miss Blake pondered everything to be done. She was filled with energy and excitement. She reflected on the journey...all the classes, her student teaching experience, so many days of substitute teaching...and she was here, now...*

*And then the question: Where do I start?*

## Connect and Reflect

Think of the day you walked into your first classroom. Allow that feeling to flood your brain.

For some of you, it's been a while and our schools probably felt very different from how they do now. For others, it was only a few years ago. And if you are reading this book in your studies to become a teacher, you've probably thought about how it will feel to walk into your first classroom.

Whatever your case may be, did you ask: *Where do I begin?*

For both seasoned and novice teachers, **the moment you question the information you have and need to design and manage your classroom is the moment you became a *teacher as architect*.**

## Our Use of the Term Effective

As you journey through this book you will come across the terms "highly effective," "effective teaching," "teacher effectiveness," "teaching effectiveness," or "effective teachers." It is important to understand and define what we mean: we measure *effectiveness* in terms of how much students learn.

Particularly over the last decade, we have been interested in **the discernible differences between good teaching in one classroom and *great* teaching in another.** To the untrained eye, and sometimes to us, it is initially hard to tell the difference. Generally, both classrooms are well managed, both teachers have a good rapport with students, and students are learning. Yet over the last 10 years, time and time again, data reveals a different story.

How can two classrooms that look the same deliver strikingly different results? In the good teacher's classroom, most students achieved a year's worth of academic growth. However, in the great teacher's classroom, most students achieved *more than* a year's worth of academic growth on summative absolute assessments—and significantly outpaced their peers on adaptive growth metrics. Why?

When we use the term effective we mean it in reference to student learning and more specifically, we mean *over one year's worth of academic growth in a school year.*

## Building a Classroom for Learning

Architects are responsible for creating customized spaces. They design a plan that is later carried out and combines specific standards that meet the needs of their clients. In the design process, architects start by being purposeful in their blueprint planning. Our observations over the years have led us to believe that our most successful teachers are very intentional in their planning. Their plans, or blueprints, have similar fundamentals. And when asked *Where Do I Begin,* all of our best teachers answered in a similar way.

Our journey together begins here.

# Why We Do What We Do

## History of Education in America

### Early History

Clayton Christensen's book, *Disrupting Class,* describes how our changing society has evolved its needs of our public schools. Christensen begins with our earliest American citizens and eloquently describes how they began to wrestle with the role schools should play. His brief primer chronicles how schools began to purposefully serve our nation—to meet the needs of its society, which in turn, will make America prosperous. He uses this analogy to introduce his concept of *disruptive innovation*—a theory that charts performance trajectories over given periods of time. Understanding how our schools have changed over time reveals why today we are again at one of those changing moments in history.

We begin considering what society has **asked** of our public schools throughout American history.

Many factors have guided and shaped the response of education throughout history. During the 1600s, 1700s, and 1800s, society asked public schools to teach the "basics," instill sound moral values, character development, and provide civic lessons to ensure a good understanding of the workings of a democracy. But the 20th century demanded new skills—motivating the public to **ask** for new kinds of education.

1600s—Education in the early United States was religious; the curriculum was based on the Bible and focused on creating good citizens who could understand and obey the common laws. It was privately funded and focused on schooling the boys of the towns. Early education in the colonies consisted of tutorials, teaching in small groups, or one-to-one apprenticeships based on a trade. Girls were educated by the women of the town on duties of the home and the Bible.

Massachusetts led the way with the founding of Boston Public Schools in 1635. The Latin Grammar School consisted of curriculum for boys ages eight to fifteen. In 1636, Harvard was founded as the first college in the United States. It began as a preparatory school for ministers and emphasized the classics of Greek and Latin studies. Although Massachusetts required teaching in all towns over 20 people, education was still focused on the elite. The concept that a common set of knowledge existed and that all children must be schooled in it only began to emerge as we entered the 18th Century.

**1700s**—In the 1700s, colonial America evolved to a changing landscape of people, government, and daily needs. The influx of people from many countries brought different religions and the purpose and needs in the classroom changed as people called for teaching of their own religious doctrines. Schools became segregated by nationality and religion. It was Thomas Jefferson who began the charge for a free accessible education for all people regardless of religion, culture, status, or sex. It took many years and much reform before this came to fruition.

**1800s**—Until the 1840s, only the wealthy could take advantage of the education system, but there were reformers such as Henry Barnard in Connecticut and Horace Mann in Massachusetts who opposed the idea of exclusiveness. When Mann published the *Common School Journal,* he brought educational concerns to the public. Reformers contended that common schooling resulted in a united society with less crime and poverty, and therefore produced good citizens. Due to the reform efforts, public elementary schooling was made available for all students by the end of the 1800s. In 1853, Massachusetts enacted the first compulsory school attendance laws.

**1900s**—It was not until the beginning of the twentieth century that public schooling was available to all students. Every state had passed compulsory school attendance legislation for the elementary level by 1918.

As America moved into the twentieth century, our society entered into an Industrial Revolution and the **ask** of our public schools shifted. This time, we needed a work force to compete with a fast-growing German economy and students needed to be trained for a vocation. However, the old methods of preparing an elite class to lead and the rest to participate in a democracy did not go away—society simply asked its schools to do both jobs. The new **ask** required the school system to extend elementary school education and offer high school to everybody. Schools expanded the curriculum and began a wide range of vocational offerings to meet the demand of a variety of industrial careers.

The rise in high school attendance was one of the most striking developments in American education during the twentieth century. From 1900 to 1996, the percentage of teenagers in the U.S. who graduated from high school increased from about 6% to about 85%. As the 20th century progressed, most states enacted legislation to extend compulsory education laws to age 16.

Participation in higher or postsecondary education in the United States also increased tremendously. The Morrill Acts of 1862 and 1890 provided federal financial support to state universities. Many land-grant colleges and state universities were established through gifts of federal land to the states for the support of higher education. Financial support was extended to the universities and this in turn led to increased research across all academic disciplines. At the beginning of the century, about 2% of Americans from the ages of 18 to 24 were enrolled in a college. Near the end of the century, more than 60% of this age group, or over 14 million students, were enrolled in about 3,500 four-year and two-year colleges.

Overall, states began assuming a more active role in public education during the 20th century. With the passage of the National Defense Education Act (1958) and the 1965 Elementary and Secondary Education Act (ESEA), Congress began to deal with issues including educating poor children and improving neglected subjects such as mathematics, science, and foreign languages. Title I of the ESEA provided funding to improve programs and educational opportunities for impoverished students. It sought to provide a path to close the achievement gap between high and low-performing children, especially the achievement gaps between minority and non-minority students, and between disadvantaged children and their more affluent peers. This struggle and challenge continues today.

Other acts include the Manpower Development and Training Act of 1963, the International Education Act of 1966, and the Vocational Act of 1963, which was passed to address educational concerns and the current needs of society. In 1975, the Education for all Handicapped Children Act was passed and has evolved into what is known today as IDEA, the Individuals with Disabilities Education Act.

Nevertheless, women were discriminated against in American schools for many years. Even in coeducational schools, practically no encouragement was given to girls. Prominent women educators who significantly contributed include Catharine Esther Beecher, Emma Willard, Mary Lyon, Jane Addams, Susan Anthony, Mrs. Carl Schurz, and Mary McLeod. These reformers established higher level institutions for women and offered subjects that earlier educators deemed unnecessary for women. The first co-educational college was Oberlin College (founded in 1833); the first enduring all-women's college was Vassar College (1861); and the first graduate school for women was at Bryn Mawr College (1880). The emergence of the women's rights movement during the 1960s was a boost against sexual discrimination. Title IX of the 1972 federal Education Amendments prohibited discrimination on the basis of sex in educational institutions that received federal aid.

## The Late 20th Century

The history and system of public education is also shaped by the significant events of the 20th century: the Great Depression, World War II, the Cold War, wars with other countries, the civil rights movement, student protests, and political events all have had their effects. In 1954, a landmark decision that we know as *Brown v Board of Education* ordered the desegregation of public schools, reversed the 1896 *Plessey v Ferguson* decision, and brought to the nation's attention the vast disparities in education between blacks and whites.

Three years later, when the Soviet Union beat the United States in launching the first satellite, Sputnik, into space, society again would ask of its public schools to do more. When the 1958 cover of *Life* Magazine declared, "Crisis in Education," this time, the ask shifted to producing graduates strong in math and science. And again, our schools responded.

This trend continued into the 1980s with *Nation at Risk: The Imperative For Educational Reform,* the 1983 report of President Ronald Reagan's National Commission on Excellence in Education. The report chronicled that America's once unchallenged dominance in commerce, industry, science, and technology was in jeopardy of being overtaken by competitors across a changing international landscape. In response to this report, most states, by the 1980s and 1990s, were giving more attention to establishing and raising expectations within public schools.

## The 21st Century and Education

As America entered the 21st century, society had another **ask** of its public schools. This time, with the passage of the 2001 No Child Left Behind Act (NCLB) it was expected that every child in every school regardless of race, economic status, language, or cognitive ability become academically proficient. The **ask** was to eliminate achievement gaps among American students, with emphasis on helping children who were living below the poverty line. NCLB was designed  to reduce bureaucracy and improve student performance by providing more public accountability. It was also designed to improve schools and teacher quality, and to give parents more flexibility in educational choices, as well as more information on their children's schools and academic performances. The early twenty-first century is understood as the Era of Accountability and Assessment Reform.

NCLB supports standards-based education reform on the belief that setting high expectations and establishing measurable goals aligned to standards can improve individual outcomes in education. The Act does not call for or provide national achievement standards; it calls for standards to be set by each individual state. NCLB became effective January 8, 2002, and has changed the way schools do business. NCLB requires all federally-funded schools to administer a yearly state-wide standardized test to all elementary through high school students. Under current legislation, each state must provide an assessment aligned to their identified state standards. Although annual standardized testing is not new to some states, being held publicly accountable for student growth and achievement was new territory. Schools must show adequate yearly progress (AYP) for all students, including minorities, the economically disadvantaged, English Language learners, and special education students. Schools now had to demonstrate that all students were learning. If schools did not meet AYP, sanctions were established and funding was jeopardized. In addition, schools had to participate in federal improvement programs and requirements.

The Act also required states and school districts to notify parents if students or the school were failing to meet the new standards. States now must provide "highly-qualified" teachers to all students, and the Act allowed parental choice in school attendance if the school was not meeting AYP or did not have highly-qualified teachers. Moreover, accountability and test scores became very public, both upping the stakes for educators and bringing more awareness to society on how our public system was performing.

## NCLB and the Critics

Criticism of the Act comes from educators, politicians, and parents. Many feel the expectation for all students to achieve a certain level is unrealistic and it is unfair and ineffective to set unachievable goals for teachers and schools. Critics claim the incentives and penalties that are built into the system can motivate schools to manipulate tests and or "teach to the test." Also, many feel that it has placed too much of an emphasis on assessments, placing unproductive stress on teachers and students. Critics believe that it has taken away from teaching of the arts and electives. Even proponents of the Act assert that the support for low performing schools is still not adequate to create real change in America's schools.

## The Charter School Movement

Charter schools provide an alternative to other public schools but are still part of the public school system. Charter schools were a response to the need for choices for parents who felt the traditional public school was not meeting their child's needs and provided a public school option to the only other choices: private school or home schooling.

The charter school movement is a reform movement at its core, with an emphasis placed on one of America's most capitalist ideologies: that only the strong will survive. Charter schools are created by parents, teachers, education reformers, and organizations who must apply through local districts, county or state offices of education.

Charter schools are attended by choice and they cannot charge tuition. Charter schools also competed with the political push for "vouchers," which is when parents seek public funding towards private school. Each state's Charter School Law outlines the state requirements and defines the process for application and granting of Charters. State laws vary but all charter schools follow two basic tenants: autonomy and accountability. The first state to pass a charter school law was Minnesota in 1991. California was second, in 1992. As of 2009, 41 states and the District of Columbia have charter school laws.

Charter schools differ from traditional public schools as they operate autonomously from the school district's policies, procedures, and requirements. Although charter schools follow policy and procedure outlined in its registered charter, including a plan for methods to monitor student achievement, charters must also meet State Standards for student growth and achievement and students must take all state-mandated assessments. Often, charters set their expectations for student achievement higher than the traditional public school.

Charter schools sought to create "ideal school programs" that could be tested, refined, and then replicated in both traditional and charter schools.

## Charter Schools—From Extreme to Mainstream

In *Understanding and Assessing the Charter School Movement,* Murphy (2002) categorizes educational reform progress into three *eras.* During the Intensification Era (1980-1987), it was believed that student outcomes were a direct result of poor classroom educators with low expectations and that there was little effort to change at the local level. Charter schools sought reform and student success through a top-down management effort that focused on policies for streamlining the use of resources, improving teacher practice, and increasing expectations.

In the Restructuring Era (1986–1995), an effort was made to correct all that was perceived wrong with the Intensification Era. Murphy sums up this problem as "Reforms did not seem to be producing the desired outcomes and the reforms were never likely to do so because they were not designed to get at the heart of the problem," (pg. 7). The focus during the Restructuring Era was to empower teachers and parents through maximizing the talent and resources at the local level.

In the Reformation Era (1992–2002), charter schools added a focus on standards reform and accountability policies. This focus aligned with the work going on in traditional public schools and federal policies for education.

Today, charter schools are commonplace and an embedded and expected part of the public school system. Many districts are modeling programs for autonomy within the system to traditional public schools showing strong student performance. The ongoing need and desire for both school choice and strong instructional accountability means that charter schools are closely linked to the market forces and in a competition to be the best. The Center for Education Reform, as of October 2010, states that 5,453 charter schools will be operating in the 2010–2011 school year, educating a record of over 1.7 million students.

## Conclusions and Implications into the 21st Century

The new **ask** of society has become not only to educate all students to higher proficiency levels (as indicated by policies like NCLB), but to produce a new workforce that can compete in a 21st century global marketplace. With the rise of the Chinese and Indian economies, new advances in technology, and a changing international landscape, America finds herself competing for both skilled and unskilled jobs.

Contemporary authors Thomas Friedman and Richard Florida have helped shape public discourse with the publication of provocative books and columns over the last decade. Friedman's *The World is Flat,* and *Hot, Flat, and Crowded* both frame America's diminishing economic and political influence in the world. Friedman's innovative policy ideas have been read by millions of readers through his columns in the *New York Times* and his blog. Friedman has been one of the loudest and most influential writers of the first decade of the 21st century about the need for our public schools to help solve this new **ask.**

Richard Florida has similarly provided a contemporary voice to the new ask, primarily around the types of skills needed to compete in the global marketplace. Florida's *The Rise of the Creative Class* and *Who's Your City* detail fascinating statistics about creative sector jobs, which are clusters of people living in close proximity involved in creative fields, and how these fields are boosting local economic activity, lifestyle choices—and happiness.

Both Florida and Friedman have challenged public schools to find solutions that simultaneously educate all students to a basic level of proficiency and produce graduates that are creative thinkers, problem solvers, analysts, synthesizers, and navigators of information. To accomplish what Florida and Friedman write about requires graduates to understand their own thinking processes. It requires our schools to explicitly teach students to have executive control over their own thinking—to know what they know and what they *don't* know. Metacognition may indeed be a critical skill that students need to solve society's new ask.

Many other contemporary authors have also weighed in on the skills our students need to compete in a global marketplace and solve society's new ask. Daniel Pink's *A Whole New Mind,* and Howard Gardner's *Five Minds for the Future* are influential works that are helping shape public debate in the early years of the 21st century. Pink argues that words like *design, story, symphony, empathy, play,* and *meaning*—all words associated with right brain activity—will be 21st century skills needed to perform jobs. Gardner argues a similar need, describing the necessary modes of the *disciplined mind, synthesizing mind, creating mind, respectful mind,* and *the ethical mind* to live and excel in a fast-paced, information-rich, and increasingly complex world.

Gardner's most recent book, *Truth, Beauty, and Goodness Reframed: Educating for the Virtues in the 21st Century,* discusses the human struggle to define the meaning of each word in his title: truth, beauty, and goodness. He eloquently describes these virtues by writing about human behaviors that lead to learning throughout life, its purpose, and the challenges associated with learning. He addresses difficult and often avoided subjects such as morality and distinguishing right from wrong, and seeks to find examples of each to illustrate his larger point.

As Florida and Friedman point us towards reasoning, creating, and metacognition as a higher-order thinking process that students need to be successful, Gardner challenges us to push the boundaries of human cognition even further, by exploring how self-actualization fits into what students should know and be able to do—given society's new **ask.**

## Guiding Questions

Every question you ask and every decision you make affects the learning outcomes for your students, and designing the best possible teaching plan starts with some more questions. The Guiding Questions part of each chapter will help guide your thinking as you experience the book.

▶ How do I *know* what students need to learn?

▶ Where do I find this information?

▶ Who determines what students should learn?

▶ How do I start the planning process?

## Connecting to Classroom Practice

As we have seen from history, defining what to teach has been largely shaped by the current needs of our society. From religious needs to producing a citizenry adept in democracy, from industrial and vocational needs to mathematical and scientific aptitude—public schools have focused on teaching the skills deemed necessary for people of that time. While the skills our students need now to compete and thrive in the 21st century may be changing, the idea that our schools teach what society needs is constant.

### Defining the *What*

WHAT we teach is multifaceted and varies across the country. We teach content in reading, writing, math, science, technology, the arts, physical education, social science, history—and through each content we teach students how to problem-solve and think.

▶ We teach students how to interact and collaborate with each other.

▶ We teach students to be creative and use all facets of their abilities to think and process.

▶ We teach content that has varied levels of specificity and depth.

▶ We teach students how to be inquisitive and to question the world around them.

Defining WHAT to teach is complicated, and then once the *what* is defined, teachers must decide HOW they will teach the *what.* Which experiences should students go through to learn the *what?* What higher-order thinking will be incorporated in the learning? How will I build the learning for my students?

Let's focus on the WHAT and how traditional public schools define at each grade level what students should know and be able to do. Every state has developed and adopted standards that identify and categorize expectations for students across grade levels and subject areas, kindergarten through 12th grade. The WHAT begins with the standards.

## The Standards

**Standards Misconception:**

*I changed grade levels, and the South Carolina State Standards won't allow me to teach my dinosaur unit this year.*

**Clarification:**

*State standards are designed for vertical articulation from kindergarten through grade 12. They seek to avoid students experiencing a duplication of standards from one grade to the next.*

### Where Do I Find My Standards?

Grade-level standards are available on state department of education websites and often on your county and district websites. Your school district should be able to offer guidance on locating copies of your grade level or content state standards and any local school district expectations. As soon as you have been assigned a grade level or subject matter to teach, begin by getting copies of the state and local standards and expectations.

## How to Read and Understand the Standards

Each state organizes standards a little differently and these documents often have specific, unique terminology. Learning about the organization and design of your specific state standards is critical. Often, standards are organized into broad statements around concepts and each standard will contain or require multiple skills to master the concept.

Some states provide additional levels that further break down the standards into learning goals, assessment frameworks, or specific skills that they will identify as power or essential standards. Terminology varies across the country. In some cases, this work is done at the district or school level in which guiding documents are created for a common understanding.

Local or district curriculum guides may further define areas of focus and or additional standards or content expectations beyond the state adopted standards. However your State standards are organized, you as the teacher must draw up or construct the plan, organizing the learning goals into units and lessons. You must clearly understand your State standards and district expectations.

## The Curriculum Trap

The word *curriculum* has long been interchangeable with "what" students will learn in school or "what" teachers will teach. However, as the teaching profession has evolved, so too has our use of the word and *curriculum* has come to mean many things to many people. This confusion sometimes muddles important conversations between educational professionals, local school boards, higher education, politicians, publishing companies, and others who would benefit from a common understanding of the term.

From the onset, clarify how *you* use the word. For the purpose of this book, we define "the WHAT" as the curriculum—or *what it is we expect students to know and be able to do.* We also believe that the curriculum includes WHAT thinking skills we want students to understand and strategically access and use. Teachers can find what students are expected to know and be able to do (the curriculum) outlined in local and state adopted standards.

**Materials Misconception:**

*When asked, "Tell me a little bit about the curriculum," the teacher responds, "Well, our curriculum is "Open Court."*

*This same teacher from Indiana is confused and angry when she finds out that the publishers aligned the scope and sequence of her new textbook to specifically address the California standards, thereby missing 15% of the Indiana standards.*

**Clarification:**

*Textbooks, commercial packaged programs, and instructional materials are not the curriculum; the State standards are the curriculum. Teachers use instructional materials like Open Court to teach the curriculum.*

There are many things that make up the curriculum and how people talk about their curriculum.

▶ Standards

▶ Thinking processes

▶ Essential questions

▶ Tasks and activities

▶ How students experience the content and thinking process

However, in isolation, people often confuse what the word actually means. Here are some common misconceptions and corresponding clarifications using the word *curriculum*.

**State Standards** are the core of a curriculum. The standards help place a concrete meaning to what we want students to know and be able to do. They tend to be broad learning goals students are expected to master and are linked to high stakes accountability tests. Most often, usually the standards are vertically-articulated from kindergarten through grade 12 and define year-end grade level expectations.

**Instructional Materials** are often provided to teachers by schools and districts. Instructional materials assist teachers in teaching the standards. Our profession's use of the word curriculum can get confusing when schools or districts buy packaged programs like *Open Court or Success for All.* Teachers follow the scope and sequence of their text and make assumptions that it is aligned to their state and local standards. Teachers often rely on the text book to tell them what to teach and do not always check that they are teaching the state and local standards. Teachers believe they are teaching all of the required state standards by using the program in its entirety.

**Methods** for how students experience the standards can also be part of curriculum mapping. However, for the purpose of this book, we have organized the pedagogical methods into a separate chapter. Curriculum maps, unit plans, and lesson plans often describe how students will experience standards.

As you can see, the word curriculum means different things to different people. Be clear about what you mean when using the word curriculum; for the purpose of this book, the curriculum or "the what" is what we want students to know and be able to do—and it begins in the state standards.

**Methods Misconception:**
*We just bought a new math curriculum. It has tons of manipulatives and hands-on activities for our students.*

**Clarification:**
*You cannot buy a curriculum; rather you can purchase instructional materials to teach the curriculum or the standards. Instructional materials often differ in both the pedagogical methods and activities and tasks for students.*

## Higher-Order Thinking Skills and the Standards

Many of you have probably been asked *what is higher-order thinking?* Higher-order thinking first appeared on the educational radar when Benjamin Bloom and his colleagues edited *A Taxonomy of Educational Goals and Objectives: Handbook I: Cognitive Domain* (1956).

While other fields had been successful at creating taxonomies and models for the purpose of classifying a body of knowledge hierarchically, this task had escaped the education profession. Bloom set out to lead this charge.

Bloom created a committee that agreed to meet yearly in the 1950s and 60s to classify educational goals and objectives to assist college examiners in writing their exams. It was the first real attempt at trying to understand thinking skills from an educator's perspective.

Much has been learned about cognition and higher-order thinking since the 1950s. New academic fields such as cognitive neuroscience have emerged and new research and studies are produced every day. Authors like Howard Gardner and Daniel Pink continue to challenge our basic assumptions about higher-order thinking and human intelligence. In coming chapters, we examine how higher-order thinking relates to standards.

We will ask you to think about your role as the classroom teacher, and how you can design plans that push students to their fullest potential and meet the needs of society's new ask.

## Blueprint Essentials

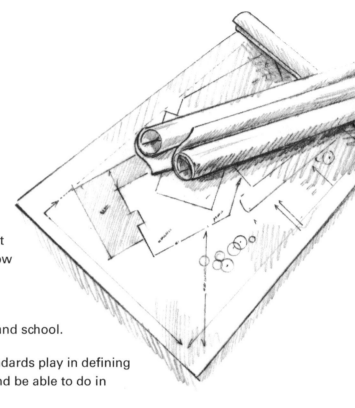

Be absolutely clear about what you want your students to know and be able to do.

Research local standards and expectations for your district and school.

Understand the role state standards play in defining what students should know and be able to do in your classroom.

The thinking we want students to do around the content drives instruction – not the text book and publishing industry.

Understand that you architect the learning in your classroom and you use instructional materials to support learning.

21st century thinking and learning is part of the curriculum and society's latest **ask.**

## Reflection and Action

▶ Think about *what* you will be teaching your students. Are you familiar with the content?

▶ What additional support might you need to understand the content better?

▶ How did learning about what society has asked of our public schools make you feel? What does it make you think about?

▶ How does society's ask affect how you think about your role as a teacher?

▶ How did reading about contemporary voices like Thomas Friedman or Howard Gardner make you think about what kids should know and be able to do?

## In the Library

### History of Education and Society

*History of Education in America* (2007)
John D. Pulliam and James J. Van Patten

### 21st Century Thinking

*A Whole New Mind* (2005)
Daniel Pink

*Five Minds for the Future* (2008)
Howard Gardner

*Truth, Beauty, and Goodness Reframed* (2011)
Howard Gardner

# Journal Entry

Now, imagine what a classroom 20 years from now might look like. Draw a picture next to your photograph of this classroom. As our journey unfolds together your visual imagery will evolve too. Give yourself permission to dream. We will tap into your imagination and creativity in the coming chapters.

**Experiencing and Personalizing your Journey**

**Physical Thinking:**
Take a picture of your classroom. Attach it here.

# Chapter 2

# Classifying Knowledge and Cognition:
## New Higher-Order Thinking in 21st Century Classrooms

*I think: therefore I am. – Descartes*

# A Teacher's Story: Extending Student Thinking

*Mr. Hsu is a high school foreign language teacher. Fluent in three languages, he teaches French and Chinese to high school students in Oregon. Today, his students are researching topics of their choice about language origins and how culture and race affected its history. His students use the internet for their research and Mr. Hsu notices similar trends in his students searching. Students seem to be collecting mostly factual information, have little patience when searching, limit their exploration to familiar websites, and have difficultly assessing the relevance of information found on the internet.*

*He is first concerned with his students' basic retrieval of information on the web. He quickly realizes that simple search and retrieval exercises won't extend his students' thinking skills, but he is unsure what to do. He consults a colleague who later asks him to reflect on the specific task assigned to his students. Mr. Hsu revisits the assignment and concludes it was too vague, lacked alignment between what he wanted his students to accomplish (objectives), the questions he posed to the class, and the thinking skills he thought would prevail while his students were engaged in the task. He decides he would try again.*

*This time, Mr. Hsu provides some parameters to the task that he believes will better align his goals and objectives with the thinking he wants students to do. Students are given a choice of topics to research, but must begin by first generating a list of possible key words to search. This will help students search for specifics, not just browse. Students must also provide the website credentials, digging deeper into who is providing the information. Students are asked to consider and analyze if their sources may have a particular bias. Students must also use multiple websites and specialized search engines like Google Scholar or Education Resources Information Center (ERIC). The task also asked students to consider differing points of view without one clear answer.*

*After conducting their research students have the choice from several web-enabled solutions: podcast, blog, wiki etc...and must create one written and one spoken report, in the foreign language, from their research. Students must also identify the purpose of their report and their target audience.*

*Later, when Mr. Hsu begins to review the student-created assignments he sees a noticeable difference in the thinking students produced from the first assignment to the second.*

## Connect and Reflect

As we read in Chapter 1, society has shaped the kinds of knowledge we want our students to master. Our instructional plan begins by knowing what to teach—and we find that information in our State standards; in a sense, those are the specs of the project. You are to build a classroom, and the State standards are the foundation upon which you are building.

As you design your classroom plan, the next step is to think about what you want your students to *do* with their new knowledge. How do you want students to think about this knowledge? Like the story above, there are many ways students can think about knowledge or content. For instance: What do the following six industries have in common?

- ▶ Animated movies
- ▶ Digital publishing
- ▶ Telephone
- ▶ Personal computer
- ▶ Tablet computing
- ▶ Music

According to biographer Walter Isaacson, these six industries were re-imagined and re-invented by Steve Jobs. Some would add a seventh, retail, in which Jobs re-imagined what retail stores looked and felt like. Jobs was responsible for some of the most innovative products over the last few decades. Steve Jobs stood at the crossroads of science and art by connecting creativity with technology. His vision and imagination

provided a roadmap for engineers to create these innovative products—
products consumers hadn't even thought of before…such as
digitally-animated movies, iBooks, iPhones, iTunes, iPads and iPods.

Teachers must find a way to design tasks that allow students' thinking to
flourish—to take them places they have never been before. One place that
can happen is at the intersection of science and technology, aesthetics and
art. Like Jobs' designs, creativity is powerfully innovative when it unites
different ways of thinking.

From the story, what connections do you make between the State standards
and higher-order thinking skills? What value would you place on one
student's ability to create an original podcast that captured the attention and
imagination of the audience—and another student's knowledge of language
origins that added insight into understanding class in the Chinese world
today? Similarly, what value would you place on your students' ability
to recall and retrieve the names and dates of the rulers of ancient China?
Or the skills needed to work at Apple?

The next section, *Why We Do What We Do,* explores how knowledge,
content, and standards are linked. We'll make the distinction between
knowledge and cognition, and frame our own learning about how
knowledge and our ability to process knowledge are linked to intelligence.
We will explore the roots of higher-order thinking by identifying those in the
education field who classified cognition into useful frameworks, models,
and taxonomies.

Lastly, in *Connecting to Classroom Practice,* we introduce our own
classification of cognition. This new classification is a tool, written to help
teachers design the type of learning experiences students will need in the
21st century. Over the course of the book we will provide you with an array
of tools to help in your blueprint design of instruction. Our journey
continues with higher-order thinking.

# Why We Do What We Do

Human reflection upon knowledge has been documented as far back as Plato and Socrates. The inquiry is germane to every era of human civilization and has been studied from the perspectives of philosophy, psychology, art, and behavioral sciences to the more recent cognitive and neurosciences. And while, at its simplest, knowledge is familiarity with an idea, a thing, or someone, we also know that there are many different types of knowledge.

## Knowledge, Content and Standards

Dochy and Alexander (1995) summarized the different types of knowledge and the ways in which we often refer to it, including: procedural, factual, declarative, conceptual, situational, disciplinary, semantic, psychomotor, socio-cultural, or strategic.

Yet in an educational setting we make the distinction between *knowledge* and *content knowledge.* Most educators think about content knowledge as specific to academic subject matter. Typically, scholars within a field come to a general consensus about the types of ideas and information believed to be necessary to be considered knowledge. Such subject-specific knowledge, or content knowledge, evolves over time as new ideas shed insight on the content.

For our purposes, we believe that *knowledge* is the generally accepted viewpoint of scholars within a specific academic discipline and that knowledge changes over time. *Content knowledge* is the result of this collective body of work or substance from the specific discipline at that moment in time. Content knowledge is identifiable by context—it is correct for its time and place, and is updated as times change. Educational content standards or State standards for a given subject are a reflection of content knowledge.

*Educational content standards or State standards for a given subject are a reflection of content knowledge.*

## Cognition and Cognitive Processing:
## Beginning Higher-Order Thinking

Knowledge is acquired through complex cognitive processing. While cognitive processing or *cognition* is the scientific term for mental processes, simply put, cognition is thinking. There are many thinking processes we use to learn new knowledge: attention, remembering or retrieving information, initial comprehending of the information, and analyzing or creating with information, all leads to knowledge.

## How Do Students Acquire Knowledge and
## What Do We Want Them To Do With It?

The ability to control and monitor our cognitive processes stems from our own metacognitive control, or our ability for *thinking about our own thinking.* We also have mental abilities to think about how we think about ourselves. We call this *self-actualization*—our ability to process and think about how everything fits together to form a concept about ourselves. How we perceive ourselves in relation to everything around us becomes part of our belief system, our values, how we define and seek happiness, our motivation for doing things, and our ability to attend to tasks.

Over the second half of the twentieth century, researchers and practitioners began an attempt to distinguish the complexity of cognitive processing. That is, some cognitive processes were thought to be lower-level, while others were considered higher level. Theories emerged about higher-order thinking and what it meant for students to be involved in tasks that demanded such thinking. For example, it's believed that higher-order thinking was characterized by the ability to perform certain mental tasks.

The following list is by no means exclusive, but intended to give an example of cognitive processing on the higher end of the spectrum.

- Visualize the problem and a potential solution
- Defend and justify solutions
- Tackle problems with more than one solution
- Separate the parts from the whole and then put them back together to form something new
- Solve a problem where the specific steps were not laid out in advance

Characterizing all of the different aspects of knowledge is beyond the intention for this chapter, let along this book. In considering the research, the complexity of the scope of the task, and the purpose of this chapter, we have decided to focus in on **four key knowledge dimensions: declarative, procedural, conceptual, and situational.**

These four dimensions are useful for teachers to classify and organize learning objectives, tasks and activities, and assessments for students. Furthermore, the knowledge dimensions we've selected represent 21st century knowledge that our students will need to navigate and be successful in the world they will inherit.

## What Is Intelligence?

Of the many ways to define intelligence, the most useful to our discussion is our ability to learn. Probably the most famous definition of intelligence to educators came in Howard Gardner's landmark 1983 book, *Frames Of Mind: The Theory of Multiple Intelligences.*

## Gardner's Multiple Intelligence Theory

Howard Gardner's *Frames of Mind* offers key insights about the argument that there are many forms of intelligence. He does so by first examining the relationship of intelligence to how the brain processes information.

Gardner identifies the problem of classifying intelligence by only using one particular lens. For example, the commonly accepted Informational Processing Theory (discussed in greater detail in chapter 5), he argues, is the theory of only a single "horizontal" problem-solving apparatus. While a single process is appealing, the carefully selected problems to which it is said to apply turn out to be, upon closer examination, disturbingly similar to one another. In common with Piagetian psychology, nearly all of the problems investigated by information-processing psychologists prove to be of the logical-mathematical sort. Gardner points out that these areas are not all associated with the informational processing mode, concluding that there are multiple forms of intelligence.

Gardner offers eloquent reasoning and examples of intelligence found in eight distinct areas.

1. Bodily-Kinesthetic
2. Interpersonal
3. Intrapersonal
4. Linguistic

5. Logical-Mathematical
6. Musical
7. Naturalistic
8. Spatial

His assertion that intelligence comes in many forms challenged early held views of intelligence. Furthermore, Gardner argues that people often have *intelligence preferences*–a hard-wired, neurological preference for thinking and learning. These preferences are unique to individuals and have implications for designing instruction in today's classrooms.

## Classifying Knowledge and Cognition: The 1956 Connection

As mentioned, during the second half of the twentieth century, theories began to emerge about higher-order thinking and classifying cognition. Probably the most influential work has its roots in 1956, when University of Chicago professor Benjamin Bloom and two colleagues edited *A Taxonomy of Educational Objectives, The Classification of Educational Goals, Handbook I: Cognitive Domain.*

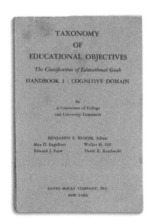

*Figure 2.1 – is a first-printing, first-edition of Handbook I from the author's collection.*

Their work began as far back as 1948 in an informal meeting at the American Psychological Association Convention in Boston, in which a group of interested participants discussed the idea of creating a theoretical framework that could be used for communication between college examiners. For the next few years, this group convened at rotating universities to classify educational objectives according to difficulty. This group attempted to discern higher-order thinking and categorized knowledge and the thinking processes into three distinct domains: cognitive, affective, and the psychomotor domain that would later become the basis for Handbook I (1956) and Handbook II (1964). The psychomotor domain was never published.

The work was a foundation stone for a new way to think about teaching and learning. Others within education have attempted to build on the original framework. Robert Mager's *Preparing Instructional Objectives* (1962) and *Gagne's Conditions of Learning* (1977) both contributed to advancing how we think about thinking.

## The 2001 Revision

In 2001, a revision of Bloom's Taxonomy was published. The editors of the updated taxonomy, Anderson et al., explicitly state two reasons for the revision:

*Figure 2.2 –* is a first-edition, first-printing of The Taxonomy of Educational Objectives, Handbook II, from the author's personal collection. It is inscribed by Bloom to the other editors.

> *First, there is a need to refocus educator's attention on the value of the original handbook, not only as an historical document but also as one that in many respects was "ahead of its time." Second, there is a need to incorporate new knowledge and thought into the framework.*

With the revision, the new group set out to revise the taxonomy for five specific purposes.

1. Increase educator understanding
2. Understand the relationship between objectives and instruction
3. Design assessments
4. Understand the concept of alignment
5. Understand the relationship between the Taxonomy Table and curriculum

The original 1956 taxonomy was a single-dimension framework that classified educational objectives according to a hierarchy of cognition. The six nouns (Knowledge, Comprehension, Application, Analysis, Synthesis, Evaluation) were thought to be a sequential order for organizing and classifying objectives, moving naturally from lower level thinking to higher-order thinking. The revised 2001 taxonomy, by contrast, is two-dimensional and classifies educational objectives by cognition and knowledge. The original nouns changed to verbs and creating was added as the highest form of thinking. The hierarchy remained as well. The two-dimensional framework is referred to as the Taxonomy Table.

While the 1956 original framework focused on the cognitive domain, it was followed in 1964 by the affective domain. Because the group never produced the psychomotor domain, in the 2001 revision, the group decided to address the problem by solely focusing on the cognitive domain. However, their placement of metacognition has been criticized. Anderson et al. concluded that by placing metacognition as a knowledge dimension "in some respects bridges the cognitive and affective domains." Yet Marzano and Kendall (2007) are quick to point out their belief that metacognition is a cognitive process and not a knowledge dimension.

## Thinking is Messier than We Thought

In a ground-breaking new work *Making Thinking Visible: How to Promote Engagement, Understanding, and Independence for All Learners* (2011), researchers Ritchhart, Church, and Morrison at Project Zero from Harvard's Graduate School of Education offer their critique of the original 1956 framework and the revised 2001 Taxonomy Table.

> *Although Bloom's categories capture types of mental activity and are thus useful as a starting point for thinking about thinking, the idea that thinking is sequential or hierarchical is problematic. Bloom suggests that knowledge proceeds comprehension, which proceeds application, and so on. However, we can find examples from our own lives where this is not the case.*

The authors go on to give an insightful example of a young child painting in which they capture and describe the child's probable mental processing. While painting, they suggest, the young artist is largely working in application mode. However, when two colors collide on the canvas, to her surprise, a new color emerges. She begins to analyze what just happened, considers this new color, and replicates the procedure. She evaluates it and finds it displeasing. When she finishes her work of art she explains to her father what happened. Her new understanding, if using both the original taxonomy and the new taxonomy, would fall on the lower levels.

Ritchhart, Church, and Morrison offer a new look at cognition, suggesting that understanding, in fact, is not a type of thinking but rather a product of and the ultimate goal of the thinking process. They further suggest that cognition is not hierarchical. Mental processing is more complex, nuanced, and messy. While thinking, we weave in and out of various mental processes (analysis, reasoning, retrieval) all with the goal of deep, expert understanding. Thus, thinking is not sequential either.

## Promoting Self-Knowledge in Schools

In 1994, Carl Rogers developed educational priorities in his book *Freedom to Learn*. Rogers was part of the humanist movement and one of a few psychologists who were concerned with experiential learning in schools. He believed that if schools nurture a child's inner being first, it will accelerate the learning of academic content knowledge. He developed priorities for schools that nurtured personal development; focused on creating a climate of trust; promoted students' positive self-esteem and concept of themselves as life-long learners; and helped students learn how to seek "a good life."

Many of Rogers' core principles are shared by Abraham Maslow. Maslow introduced the idea of a *hierarchy of needs,* a path humans follow which concludes with individuals seeking to become *self-actualized* human beings. He writes, in *Toward a Psychology of Being* (1968), that certain needs—physiological, safety, belonging, and esteem needs—must be met before students can learn academic content knowledge. His four basic "deficiency needs" must be met before the individual is able to attend to their "being needs." The being needs address cognitive, aesthetic, and self-actualizing needs. His writings, along with Rogers', have influenced our thinking about the types of needs our students in the 21st century require—and how we as educators can design curriculum and instruction to meet those needs.

Since then, other educators have contributed to shaping the taxonomy. The most recent of these are Robert Marzano and John Kendall, who wrote *The New Taxonomy of Educational Objectives,* 2007, 2nd edition. In their work, they build on the 1956 framework by creating a model of behavior that describes how humans make decisions to engage in a task, and explain how information is processed once the task is underway. This model was then translated, like the 2001 revision, into a new two-dimensional taxonomy. However, the authors are quick to point out the differences. In their words:

> *First, it presents a model or theory of human thought as opposed to a framework. Technically, models and theories are systems that allow one to predict phenomena; frameworks are loosely organized sets of principles that describe characteristics of given phenomena but do not necessarily allow for the prediction of phenomena.*

By this definition, Bloom's taxonomy of 1956 is a *framework.* By designing a model first, Marzano and Kendall argue that they have truly created a hierarchical model of the flow of information processing, beginning first with the self-system's decision to engage in a new task, the meta-cognitive system's monitoring and goal setting of the new task, and the cognitive system's execution of processing the information within the new task.

Marzano and Kendall also point out that the original 1956 framework makes no distinction between knowledge and cognition. Even the original authors acknowledge this omission when they described *Level 1.0 Knowledge* of the taxonomy and the various types within. Often mistaken for *remembering or retrieval,* the original taxonomy mixed knowledge and cognition. There are still other differences; the 2007 Marzano and Kendall work combines the cognitive, affective, and psychomotor and the 2001 revision of Bloom only addresses cognitive processing. Anderson's group recognized this problem.

Marzano and Kendall furthermore developed their new model and taxonomy for five specific purposes.

1.  Classify educational objectives

2.  Design assessments

3.  Redesign state and district standards

4.  Curriculum design

5.  Thinking skills within the curriculum

In 1956, the original group acted on the need for a new taxonomy to help educators create educational objectives. It has been 10 years since the 2001 revision of Bloom's Taxonomy and nearly five years since Marzano and Kendall's publication.

## Guiding Questions

▶ Are more changes to the educational taxonomy necessary to reflect how we now understand thinking?

▶ What is higher-order thinking?

▶ Has higher-order thinking changed over the years?

▶ Who is responsible for teaching higher-order thinking?

▶ Is higher-order thinking embedded in the standards?

▶ What is the difference between rigor and higher-order thinking skills?

# Connecting to Classroom Practice

In researching this book, we surveyed the literature from the last 100 years about how educators have thought about the role knowledge and cognition play in American schooling. We also took into account contemporary voices like Thomas Friedman, Daniel Pink, Richard Florida, and Howard Gardner and synthesized their viewpoints about the current and future state of our public school system. In doing so, we've created what we hope will be a useful, practical base of knowledge for teachers—to help in your own design of curriculum and instruction.

## Teacher as Architect: Our Cognitive Targets

Our *Cognitive Growth Targets* help classify the cognitive skills students need in the 21st century. We intentionally use the word targets rather than framework, theory, taxonomy, or model for several distinct purposes. By target we mean a fixed goal or objective, or a thing at which an action or remark is directed. Our targets are intended to be a guide for teacher planning. At the core, our Cognitive Growth Targets are the convergence of principles from Bloom's cognitive domain and affective domain, the inclusion of ideas from Roger and Maslow, and new insights from the field of cognitive neuroscience.

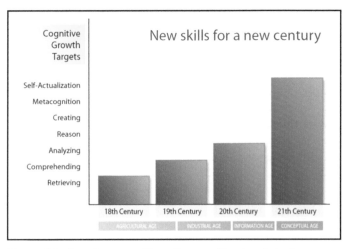

*Figure 2.3 – is a diagram of how the cognitive levels in the Cognitive Growth Targets track against the evolving skills required from students across the centuries.*

Some might say our targets represent *conative* skills. In other words, our targets combine how one thinks (cognition) with how one feels (affective). When taken together, these are often referred to as conative skills. It is precisely this intersection where we believe 21st century skills are needed in curriculum, instruction, and assessment.

Our targets are not designed to be sequential. As such, our targets differ from both works of Bloom's Taxonomy (1956) and (2001). Reasoning may occur as a result of retrieving prior knowledge, which in turn, may lead to an analysis of the information, then a summary, before an act of creating. In such a case, the cognitive processes are not happening in a sequential order. We believe that the young artist, as described in the Project Zero study, had thinking processes that moved in and out of the Cognitive Growth Targets—just as they are intended to. However, our targets are hierarchical in that they differ in complexity; in this case, Ritchhart, Church, and Morrison might suggest this to be problematic, as they did with Bloom's Taxonomy.

Additionally, we have included *comprehending* as a form of cognition, rather than a product of it. While Ritchhart, Church, and Morrison make a compelling argument for understanding as a result of cognition, we believe that a more basic, initial form of understanding happens as a *thinking process.* We call this comprehending.

Wherever you may fall on the continuum of classifying cognition, our message to teachers is to be deliberate in the types of thinking you want students to do. Having targets assist teachers in intentionally designing tasks and activities that get at student thinking and learning. Students must be given opportunities to think about content in many ways and our Cognitive Growth Targets will help you classify some of those ways.

| Research: Key Principles in How Cognitive Growth Targets Were Developed | |
|---|---|
| **Bloom 1956 Handbook I: Cognitive Domain** | **Knowledge** is the remembering of previously learned material. <br><br> **Comprehension** is the ability to grasp the meaning of material. <br><br> **Application** refers to the ability to use learned material in new and concrete situations. <br><br> **Analysis** refers to the ability to break down material into its component parts so that its organizational structure may be understood. <br><br> **Synthesis** refers to the ability to put parts together to form a new whole. <br><br> **Evaluation** is concerned with the ability to judge the value of material for a given purpose. |
| **Krathwohl 1964 Handbook II: Affective Domain** | **Receiving:** Awareness, willingness to hear, selected attention. <br><br> **Responding:** Active learner participation. Attends and reacts to a particular phenomenon. Learning outcomes may emphasize compliance in responding, willingness, or satisfaction in responding. <br><br> **Valuing:** The worth or value a person attaches to a particular object, phenomenon, or behavior. <br><br> **Organization:** Organizes values into priorities by contrasting different values, resolving conflicts between them and creating a unique value system. <br><br> **Characterization:** Has a value system that controls their behavior. The behavior is pervasive, consistent, predictable and most importantly, characteristic of the learner. |
| **Rogers Experiential Learning** | Emphasized including feelings and emotions in education. A true learning facilitator should have the following characteristics and behaviors: <br><br> **Realness:** Instructors should not present a facade but should strive to be aware of their own feelings and to communicate them in the classroom context. The instructor should present genuineness and engage in direct personal encounters with the learner. <br><br> **Prizing the Learner:** This characteristic includes acceptance and trust of each individual student. The instructor must be able to accept the fear, hesitation, apathy and goals of the learner. <br><br> **Empathic Understanding:** The instructor can understand student reactions from the inside. |
| **Maslow's Hierarchy of Needs** | **Self-actualization:** Being self-aware, concerned with personal growth, less concerned with the opinions of others and interested in fulfilling their potential. <br><br> **Esteem:** The need for self-esteem, personal worth, social recognition and accomplishment. <br><br> **Belongingness:** The need for belonging, love and affection. <br><br> **Safety:** The need for safety and security. <br><br> **Physiological:** The most basic needs that are vital to survival: water, air, food and sleep. |

Students need new skills to meet the new social ask. We believe the Cognitive Growth Targets help message to educators the kinds of tasks we should be designing for students to help them succeed in tomorrow's even more complex world. Use the Cognitive Growth Targets to design instruction for 21st century skills. They can lay the framework to analyze and plan for:

▶ Improving lessons and questioning in relation to necessary higher-order thinking skills

▶ How the learner will internalize the curriculum or the learner's affect toward the content

▶ How the learner will relate emotionally to the lesson or content

▶ How the learner will be motivated by and react to the content

**Cognitive Growth Targets** can help teachers in other ways:

▶ Classify learning objectives

▶ Design assessments

▶ Create instructional alignment

▶ Operationalize the new Common Core State standards

▶ Create useful and practical tools for educators

Additionally, the Targets help teachers develop curriculum for today's students that address:

▶ Analysis, reasoning and creating in real-world contexts

▶ Students' own thinking processes (metacognition)

▶ Students' own understanding of themselves (self-actualization)

Most importantly, understand that the purpose of the Target is to weave in and out—unlike a bull's-eye, where hitting the center every time is the goal—this Target is designed to track student thinking by aligning curriculum, instruction, and assessment.

We have selected four types of knowledge, all often classified as standards: **declarative, procedural, conceptual,** and **situational.**

---

### Knowledge Dimensions

**Declarative** knowledge is knowing facts and information.

**Procedural** knowledge is knowing how to do something.

**Conceptual** knowledge is knowing relationships between things or within a larger structure.

**Situational** knowledge is knowing a particular situation.

---

The first three types of knowledge are commonly taught in schools to organize educational objectives, examine questions, and create tasks and assessments for students. The fourth, *situational knowledge,* has not been a focus in 20th century education, but deserves a place in the schooling of 21st century students. Today's students will increasingly need knowledge and skills that require adaptability, flexibility, collaboration, and the ability to read a situation in the moment. Situational knowledge is often embedded in language, culture, or traditions. Today's world is interconnected and diverse and our students will need to learn how to interact within it.

*Cognitive Growth Targets:* Processes of Thinking

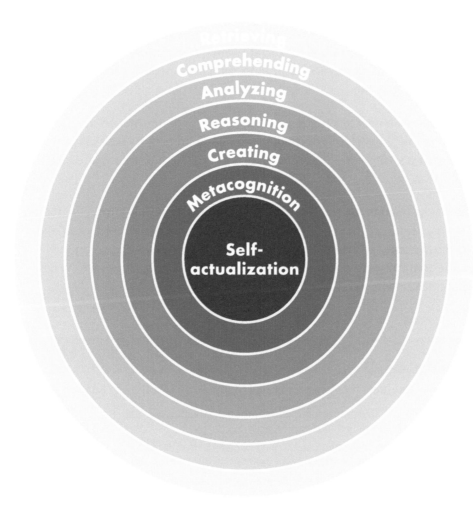

## Retrieving

Using our Targets, the simplest form of cognition is one's ability to remember or recognize something familiar. We often call this *retention* or *retrieval.* Retrieving is the process of recalling or recognizing declarative, procedural, or conceptual knowledge from memory. Memorization used to be an important skill valued by society. When books and print materials were rare and harder to access, memorizing information played a critical role in everyday life.

However, with new technologies, swiftly-changing information updates through many new types of media, and nearly immediate access to internet information, retrieving memorized information isn't as necessary as it once was.

Tasks designed to have students memorize and retrieve information should be purposeful and have a larger meaning behind it, which is why retrieving forms the outer space on our target. When planning and designing your classroom instruction, be thoughtful about learning objectives and tasks that ask students to retrieve information.

| Examples of Retrieving and Memorization | |
| --- | --- |
| **Sample *Questions* for Use During Close Readings:**<br><br>What sentence tells you what the first problem was that the main character faced in the story?<br><br>Can you **identify** a contradiction in a character's behavior from the story? What specific words does the author use to make her point?<br><br>What is the setting of the story? What sentence tells you this?<br><br>How old is the main character? What paragraph provided this evidence for you? | **Action Words**<br><br>Recall<br>Recognize<br>Label<br>Record<br>Identify<br>Define<br>Describe<br>Arrange<br>Match<br>Reproduce<br>Name<br>State<br>Illustrate |
| **Tasks and Activities:**<br><br>Illustrate a 1776 map of the United States by first studying the map in your textbook.<br><br>Reproduce the picture American Gothic. Name the artist.<br><br>Use the vocabulary words from the chapter to describe the main character. | |

## Comprehending

Moving beyond retrieval requires the brain to shift from remembering or recognizing knowledge to a more meaningful kind of learning. We call this *transfer*. Transfer requires a more complex form of cognition and starts with our ability to understand something.

Comprehension is the process of initial understanding of declarative, procedural, or conceptual knowledge and is the second of our outer rings on the target.

*Be deliberate in the building of instruction. In our observations of thousands of teachers over the years, we have found that without intentional planning, instruction rarely moves from comprehending of material to analysis, reasoning, or creating.*

| Examples of Comprehending | |
|---|---|
| **Sample *Questions* for Use During Close Readings:**<br><br>In paragraph 4, how do the following vocabulary words _____ and _____ relate to each other?<br><br>Can you **summarize** the last paragraph by putting it into your own words?<br><br>**Compare** the author's use of the word principle in the first paragraph with the use of the word principal in the second paragraph. What do you notice?<br><br>When the author says, " INSERT ANY TEXT", **explain** what you think the author is trying to say. | **Action Words**<br><br>Summarize<br>Explain<br>Cite<br>Estimate<br>Apply<br>Execute<br>Associate<br>Group<br>Compare<br>Predict<br>Discuss<br>Infer<br>Order<br>Constrast<br>Extend |
| **Tasks and Activities:**<br><br>Compare a map of the U.S. in 1776 with a map of the U.S. after the War of 1812. Note the similarities and differences.<br><br>Use the vocabulary words from the chapter to infer how the main character might respond to her mother. | |

Analyzing

As we move inward on the target, the cognitive processes demand more complex forms of thinking. These more demanding forms of cognition are often associated with the skills needed to negotiate the 21st century's endless flow of information, as well as the critical skills necessary to live more productive and fulfilling lives and earn higher wage jobs. *Analyzing* is the process of examining knowledge by breaking it down into components to determine relationships, structure, and/or purpose.

| Examples of Analyzing | |
|---|---|
| **Sample *Questions* for Use During Close Readings:**<br><br>In the final paragraph, the author chose to put the word "maybe" in quotes to draw attention to it.<br><br>Why do you think he chose to do this? What lesson do you think he wants his readers to connect with?<br><br>Why do you think the author does not reveal the main character's illness until the end of the story? What sentence supports your point of view?<br><br>The main character's father never appears in the story.<br>Why do you think the author chose to do this? Was it intentional? Why or why not?<br><br>**Organize** the 4 lessons the main character learned on their journey through the forest in order of importance. How would you determine which is the most important? Use specific evidence from the text to support your decision. | **Action Words**<br><br>Select<br>Separate<br>Organize<br>Breakdown<br>Examine<br>Outline<br>Prioritize<br>Classify |
| **Tasks and Activities:**<br><br>What is your opinion on why sharks do not attack dolphins? Prioritize the main reasons why.<br><br>**Organize** the events in the aftermath of the earthquake over a period of one hour; find evidence that supports how these events saved thousands of lives. | |

## Reasoning

Reasoning is the process of drawing conclusions or making judgments based upon evidence, facts, or criteria.

| Examples of Reasoning | |
| --- | --- |
| **Sample *Questions* for Use During Close Readings:**<br><br>**Evaluate** the approach that the main character took to find the truth about her mother. Would you have done the same thing? Defend why or why not.<br><br>When the protagonist says, "INSERT TEXT", **critique** their message from the antagonist's point of view. What specific words does the author use to make her point?<br><br>What sentence best **justifies** why the main character reacted the way he did at the end of the story? | **Action Words**<br><br>Critique<br>Interpret<br>Plan<br>Hypothesize<br>Test<br>Combine<br>Evaluate<br>Check<br>Defend<br>Integrate<br>Judge<br>Justify<br>Generalize<br>Prove |
| **Tasks and Activities:**<br><br>**Combine** all responses the class gave in the survey and provide the group with a general statement.<br><br>**Hypothesize** how chemical A will react with chemical B and then test your hypothesis. | |

## Creating

Creating, the process of making, inventing, or producing something new, is often considered the highest form of mental functioning. Today, we can point to many examples of the mental process of creating in our culture. For instance, take for example New York City, Los Angeles, and Nashville— three American cities thriving from economic activity in the arts. A walk down Broadway in New York, a visit to one of hundreds of film and television studios in Los Angeles, or a tour of a country music recording studio in Nashville serve as great examples of the flourishing business of creating in the arts industry. Another American hot spot for creating is Silicon Valley, where scientists, engineers, and artists move to be part of the technology revolution.

Yet, while the act of creating seems to be part of the backbone of the American competitiveness, American schooling has been slow to adopt this viewpoint. Policies and practices in our schools have taken a sharp u-turn from the examples listed above. Our public schools have sought to standardize the curriculum, make multiple-choice testing pervasive, and offer an industrialized model of school by mass producing, in an assembly line approach, productive citizens.

*We believe it is possible to use standards as our roadmap, but to generate tasks and activities for students that extend student thinking past rote memorization and retrieval. Today's classrooms must cultivate students' natural curiosity and provide opportunities for students to synthesize and create. Teachers must be explicit in their planning to use open-ended questions, pose problems that have more than one solution, or present real-world simulations that students will respond to.*

## Examples of Creating

**Sample *Questions* for Use During Close Readings:**

If you could change the last paragraph to alter the ending of the story what would you change?

Rewrite the last paragraph to **create** a new ending.

**Invent** a new character that would complement the theme of the story. Add the character into one of the scenes.

**Tasks and Activities:**

Currently, congressmen and women are allowed to hold office for an unlimited amount of terms. **Propose** a new congressional election model for the future and generate a communications plan for how you will sell this to the people of the United States.

**Design** a product that takes parts from both Apple and Android technologies to **create** a new device.

**Action Words**

Design
Develop
Generate
Construct
Invent
Plan
Adapt
Transform
Produce
Compose
Create
Propose

## Metacognition

Metacognition is the process of being aware of and monitoring one's own thinking and learning. Probably more than anything else, schooling today needs to teach students to think and this begins by helping children become aware of their own thinking and learning. Today's students must be metacognitive thinkers.

There are many ways teachers can do this. One way to embed this Growth Target into your lessons is by leveraging *reflection*. Students must learn to reflect often. This starts by intentionally planning moments for student reflection in every lesson. Reflection helps draw closure to lessons, reinforces key concepts and big ideas, and teaches students to begin monitoring their own thinking and learning.

> ***Metacognition***
> **Action Words**
>
> Consciousness
> Planning
> Intentional
> Reflection
> Choice(s)
> Thinking
> Learning
> Wonder
> Goals

Students should be given opportunity to demonstrate their understanding of content through performance and then they should be asked to think about their academic mistakes. This type of mental task helps students retrace their thinking and begins to help students form strategies for solving problems. It also creates thinking stamina.

It takes a disciplined mind to be aware of, monitor, and leverage our own thinking. In Howard Gardner's 2009 *Five Minds for the Future,* he writes, "Students may have accumulated plenty of factual or subject matter knowledge, but they have not learned to think in a disciplined way." To do so will require teachers to intentionally plan for students to think about their own thinking—to make tasks relevant and real-world and to make sure that the reflection has meaningful significance in students' lives.

## Self-Actualization

Self-actualization is the process of understanding one's self. We include this Target to emphasize the importance of, and our role in, helping students develop into well-rounded, fulfilled human beings. Self-actualization in curriculum development began in the 1960s and 70s with the humanist movement in psychology, and was documented by Bloom's taxonomy.

Bloom's original 1956 *Handbook I* focused on the cognitive domain, while the 1964 *Handbook II* focused on the affective domain. What makes this particular Target unique is that it's a combination of principles from several schools of thought. Key elements from both *Handbook I* and *II*, plus contemporary voices like Howard Gardner's 2011 *Reframing Truth, Beauty, and Goodness* have converged to help teachers think about designing curriculum and instruction for 21st century students.

We intentionally include key attributes of the affective domain: students' feelings, attitudes, beliefs, their capability to respond to a call when needed, willingness to express appreciation for others, ability to make life-affirming choices, or desire to follow ethical or moral standards. We also include key elements of motivation theory and the role that attention plays in high-level cognition.

Pulling from leading authorities in contemporary psychology, we examined Gardner's 2011 insights about goodness. We surveyed his work for questions about what it means to be good in this new, interconnected world. He suggests that schools create a "Set of common spaces where reflective individuals can describe the dilemmas that arise at work or in their civic roles, how they have dealt with them, how they might behave differently in the future."

Gardner's vision is a compelling idea—that as part of our schooling, adults and students should discuss moral and ethical issues together, and debating respectfully, arrive at a moral consensus.

## Self-Esteem and Self-Efficacy

Planet Earth is fast-approaching eight billion people, all of whom have diverse cultures and viewpoints about how to behave in this world we share. As the world "flattens," our students will need the necessary emotional skills to navigate an increasingly complex global society, all the while trying to find their own place in it.

The terms *self-efficacy* and *self-esteem* are related to self-actualization. Self-efficacy refers to a student's belief about their ability to succeed, while self-esteem is how students feel about themselves. Education should help students think about other questions in life and how they relate to learning in the content areas. The following questions can start discussion:

| **Self-Esteem and Self-Efficacy Action Words** |
| :---: |
| Morals |
| Hope |
| Emotion |
| Happiness |
| Community |
| Acceptance |
| Empathy |
| Fulfillment |
| Ethics |
| Introspect |
| Perspective |
| Attention |
| Beliefs |
| Control |
| Global |
| Purpose |
| Motivation |
| Citizenry |
| Joy |

▶ Who am I?

▶ Why am I here?

▶ What was I born to do?

▶ What is the meaning and purpose of my life?

▶ How do I increase my capacity for love and joy?

▶ What motivates me?

▶ How will I make the world a better place?

▶ How will I give back to my community?

These questions are about exploring the self, and the better we as teachers understand and fulfill our role in guiding students towards an increased self-understanding of their place in the world, the better we prepare them for its challenges.

## The Power of Story

Exploring the meaning of story with students can be a powerful way to help them explore who they are and to help them think about meaning in their own lives. The use of a continuously re-examined personal narrative as a year-long project is one way to think about achieving this growth target. When we teach students that story is an integral part of the human experience it has a unique opportunity to help them find meaning in their lives, both with the stories we tell about ourselves and with the stories we tell about other people. We are our stories—the narrative of our experiences, feelings, emotions, dreams, fears. Story provides a pathway for teachers to explore, with students, self-actualization and the search for understanding within themselves.

There are many practical ways to use story in your classroom. As we explore in Chapter 6, many Web 2.0 tools exist to document story in a compelling way for students. Think about ways for students to describe and reflect upon their personal narrative in the context of their lives and in relation to the content they are learning.

## Cognitive Growth Targets Poster

**COGNITIVE** GROWTH TARGETS™

**Retrieving:** The process of recalling and/or recognizing declarative, procedural, or conceptual knowledge from memory.

**Comprehending:** The process of initial understanding of declarative, procedural, or conceptual knowledge.

**Analyzing:** The process of examining knowledge by breaking it down into its components to determine relationships, structures, and/or purpose.

**Reasoning:** The process of drawing conclusions and/or making judgments based upon evidence, facts, or criteria.

**Creating:** The process of making, inventing, or producing something new.

**Metacognition:** The process of being aware of one's own thinking and learning.

**Self-actualization:** The process of understanding one's self.

Copyright © 2012 Modern Teacher Press. All rights reserved.

## Blueprint Essentials

Cognition is the process of thinking.

The types of thinking society requires from its skilled labor force has increased in complexity over the centuries.

Education first began to classify educational objectives with higher-order thinking in the late 1940's. Bloom's Taxonomy was first published in 1956. Other models have since followed.

The Cognitive Growth Targets were designed to classify 21st century thinking and help teachers align educational objectives, questions, tasks, activities, and assessments. It is the new higher-order thinking.

## Reflection and Action

▶ Do you remember studying Bloom's Taxonomy in your teacher preparation courses? What has changed? Are you familiar with the 2001 revision?

▶ How will the Cognitive Growth Targets help you in your planning?

▶ How often do students in your classroom engage in tasks and activities aligned to reasoning and creating? What does learning look like when this happens? Are students more engaged?

# In the Library

## Classifying Cognition

*A Taxonomy of Educational Objectives,*
*The Classification of Educational Goals: Cognitive*
*Domain Handbook I* (1956)
Benjamin Bloom

*A Taxonomy of Educational Objectives,*
*The Classification of Educational Goals: Affective*
*Domain Handbook II* (1964)
David Krathwohl

*A Taxonomy for Learning, Teaching and Assessing:*
*A Revision of Bloom's Taxonomy of Educational*
*Objectives (2001)*
Lorin W. Anderson, et al. (David R. Krathwohl,
Peter W. Airasian, Kathleen A. Cruikshank, Richard E.
Mayer, Paul R. Pintrich, James Raths, Merlin C. Wittrock)

## Classifying Intelligence

*Frames of Mind: The Theory of Multiple*
*Intelligences* (latest edition)
Howard Gardner

# Journal Entry

**Experiencing and
Personalizing your Journey**

What positive learning experience do you remember most from your childhood? Did it take place in school? Why was it such a positive experience for you?

In the space provided, describe your most memorable (positive) learning experience. Use the Cognitive Growth Targets to analyze the thinking you were asked to do as a result of the learning experience. What connections can you make between the learning experience, the thinking you were engaged in, and the Cognitive Growth Targets?

# Chapter 3

# Understanding
## Common Core
## State Standards

# A Teacher's Story

*Mrs. Washington teaches 4th grade in Southern California. It is January, and everybody just returned from winter break, and she is excited to see her students. It is the time of year that fourth graders really start to show both academic and social growth. Things really start to connect and they are becoming much more analytical and deeper thinkers. She looks at her instructional calendar, noting that in two weeks it will be time to administer her second quarter reading diagnostics. Mrs. W reflects on her class and instructional plans to date. She feels good about her class progress and although she has a few students who are below benchmark standards in reading, she reassures herself that her intervention plan has been in motion and she has been systematically giving support to these students. She anticipates that all of her students will show growth on the upcoming district reading assessment, including her intervention group and she predicts that two of the students in the group will even have made enough progress to meet January benchmarks.*

*A week later Mrs. W gets notice that she has a new student: Samuel and his family have moved from Iowa to California. She quickly prepares her family welcome documents and name tags for Samuel's desk. A new student is always exciting but leads to questions: How will Samuel adjust to his new classroom? To the move? How is his social and emotional development to date? How is he performing academically? What are his likes and dislikes?... so many unknowns.*

*Mrs. W receives assessment data from Samuel's school in Iowa which indicate that his reading skills meet expectations and that his math skills are above average. His first quarter report card indicates the same and that he is a happy, confident student. Samuel joins Room 10 and makes new friends easily. Mrs. W sees concerns with his reading skills within the first few days and she administers her districts reading diagnostic assessment right away. It reveals that Samuel has strong phonics and letter recognition skills but both his fluency and comprehension skills are below benchmark for fourth graders in January. She creates an intervention plan and invites his mother to come in and discuss implementation. Mrs. W shares the*

*types of interventions Sam will participate in at school and they discuss
activities they can do at home to assist Samuel in developing his fluency
and comprehension skills. She asked Mrs. Washington, why did Sam's
old school indicate that he was on track in reading? Mrs. Washington had
wondered that herself. She responded by explaining that each state has
different standards and reading benchmarks. She reassured Sam's
mother that together they would help Samuel catch up and be ready to
meet benchmarks for the California state assessments coming up in May.*

*Why is it that Sam could read in one state but not in another state?*

## Connect and Reflect

Like many of you, when we began teaching, standards weren't in
common practice and weren't yet a federal mandate. What students
needed to know and be able to do at each grade level was a local decision
and varied from district to district, school to school, and even from
classroom to classroom within the same building and same grade level.

### The Ask: Standards

State standards and assessments are now regulated through a federal
mandate, and student learning expectations and assessments are
determined by each state, and must meet NCLB regulations. Yet the origin
of the standards movement is fundamentally from society's **ask** of
education. The ask of the last decade was to meet the educational needs
of all students, regardless of race or poverty; this ask led to mandated
state systems of accountability for standards and student achievement.
Proof of compliance and growth are now linked to public school funding.

Society's **ask** of education in the first decade of the 21st century has
been refined even further, starting with educators, parents, politicians,
and philanthropists questioning: Why is an education in Mississippi so
different from that in California—and why is that so different from
Massachusetts? Furthermore, our society has begun to question the
types of skills our students need to compete in a global economy. In this
second decade of the 21st century, we see a new movement. Should the
standards and the evaluation of mastery vary from state to state?

# Why We Do What We Do

The standards movement evolved in 2009 with the Common Core Initiative, which offers states an option to adopt a common set of standards from kindergarten through high school (K–12) in English Language Arts and Mathematics. This initiative is not a federal- or national-led effort but rather comes from the states for the states. By the end of 2011, 46 of the 50 states and the District of Columbia, including the American territory of the Virgin Islands adopted the Common Core State Standards (CCSS). At the time of printing, the following states and territories have not adopted the CCSS: Alaska, Nebraska, Texas, Virginia, American Samoa Islands, Guam, Puerto Rico, and Northern Mariana Islands.

## The Common Core State Standards

The Common Core State Standards Initiative was coordinated by the National Governors Association Center for Best Practices (NGA Center) and the Council of Chief State School Officers (CCSSO). The standards were developed in collaboration with teachers, school administrators, and experts and designed to provide a clear and consistent pathway to prepare students for college and the workforce. The Common Core State Standards were based on the most effective models from states across the country as well as from countries around the world.

The CCSS are designed to provide teachers and parents with a common understanding of what students are expected to learn, *regardless of where they live in the United States.* They differ from state standards because they provide a consistent set of core standards with benchmarks of learning for all students. Common standards were established to help ensure that students are receiving a consistent high quality education, from school to school and state to state.

**YOUR State's Standards**

*90% of states have adopted the **Common Core State Standards (CCSS)**. This chapter examines and illustrates how to read and understand these standards.*

*The skills and concepts used to break standards down can be applied to any set of State standards in any subject. Be familiar with and understand the **organization and language** of your State's (and any local) standards.*

We have already begun to see that the Common Core State Standards provide (and will continue to create) a greater opportunity to share experiences and best practices across the country—which in turn improves our ability to serve students.

English language arts and math were the first subjects chosen by the Common Core State Standards coalition because these two subjects provide skills that students use to build additional skill sets in other subject areas. They are also the subjects most frequently assessed for accountability purposes.

Yet the other subject areas such as science, social studies, history, physical education, and the arts are critical to young people's education and successful development. Most states that have adopted the Common Core State Standards continue to use their adopted state standards in science and the social sciences. States that have created and adopted standards in physical education and the arts also use them along with the Common Core.

If your state has not adopted the Common Core, then it will have state-adopted standards for you to follow. Each state adoption is unique. Understanding the design and language of your state's system is the first step in determining the specifications of what you need to design instruction for your classroom.

## Guiding Questions

▶ Has my state adopted the CCSS? What are my state standards? Are there any local or district standards that I need to use?

▶ How will CCSS affect my teaching? How will I gain a deeper understanding of the CCSS?

▶ How will CCSS change learning outcomes for students?

▶ How will I assure that I am teaching the "thinking" part of the CCSS?

# Connecting to Classroom Practice

The Common Core State Standards for English Language Arts (ELA) articulate rigorous grade-level expectations in the areas of reading, writing, speaking, listening, and language. They are designed to prepare all students to be college and career ready (CCR). The Common Core State Standards will provide a vehicle for all educators to re-think teaching and learning and engage in dialogue about the skills and experiences students need to have in school to succeed and compete in the global landscape of the 21st century. There are key shifts built into the development of the CCSS based on gaps in the current system seen over time and based on the new challenges and skills needed in this new century. CCSS initiative seeks to fill the gaps in areas of rigor and content as well as meet the needs of society's future. These shifts are being discussed across the education communities in America and beyond as districts begin to implement the CCSS. Three key changes being highlighted within the ELA CCSS are:

▶ Building knowledge through content rich nonfiction.

▶ Reading, writing, and speaking from evidence grounded in literary and informational text.

▶ Regular practice with complex text to develop skill, concentration, and stamina to understand and analyze its academic language.

These shifts highlight the difference between our current practice and the change needed to meet the level of rigor required in the Common Core.

## Key Change One:
## Building knowledge through content-rich nonfiction

The CCSS emphasize a 50:50 balance of informational and literary text at the elementary level and 75:25 at the secondary level. This shift is important because the majority of reading that takes place in both college and within the workplace is informational text. By increasing the informational text in our classrooms, teachers help to provide students with access to the world around them through text. Gaining knowledge is one of the most influential factors in reading comprehension and an emphasis on informational text provides a unique opportunity for students to learn about history, science and the arts through careful study and collaboration using informational text.

## Key Change Two:
## Reading, writing and speaking grounded in evidence from informational and literary text

Students are frequently asked de-contextualized prompts such as,

> *"Do you feel that requiring students to wear uniforms in school is justified? Why or why not?"*

Prompts like these, even if paired with some type of article or passage about school uniforms do not require students to closely read the text to find evidence. Many classroom discussions and tasks currently use text as a jumping off point to talk about other things including students prior experiences. In contrast, the first anchor standard in the Common Core expects students to:

> *"read closely to determine what the text says explicitly and to make logical inferences from it; cite specific textual evidence when writing or speaking to support conclusions drawn from the text."*

This does not mean that we will never ask students about their own experiences, but the CCSS will require that we teach students to understand, analyze, and be connected to the text in reading, writing, and speaking. This skill begins in the kindergarten standards and continues through the common core high school standards.

## Key Change Three:
## Regular practice with complex text and its academic language

The ACT, *Reading between the Lines,* study conducted in 2006, played a large part in the direction of the Common Core. This study noted that only 51 percent of students are prepared for college level reading. After further research, the report showed that what set students apart was not their ability to determine the main idea or an author's message successfully; but moreover, it was the student's ability to read and analyze more complex texts. Appendix A states:

> *Being able to read complex text independently and proficiently is essential for high achievement in college and the workplace and important in numerous life tasks. Moreover, current trends suggest that if students cannot read challenging texts with understanding— if they have not developed the skill, concentration, and stamina to read such texts—they will read less in general. In particular, if students cannot read complex expository text to gain information, they will likely turn to text-free or text-light sources, such as video, podcasts, and tweets. These sources, while not without value, cannot capture the nuance, subtlety, depth, or breadth of ideas developed through complex text. (CCSS, 2010, Appendix A, p. 4)*

The call for students to practice regularly with sufficiently complex, grade level text will change teachers' choices in the classroom and continually push for both balance in text choices and rigor in our ELA classrooms.

So what does this mean for my classroom? How will I understand and address this when teaching with the new standards? Let's begin with the organization of the new standards and how to read them; understanding the organization and new language of the common core is important as you engage in discussion with colleagues and begin to implement them in your classroom.

# Common Core State Standards Design: ELA

The following are key design features in the ELA Common Core State Standards (CCSS). English Language Arts Standards are broken into two types: ***College and Career Ready/Anchor Standards and Grade-Level Specific Standards.***

## College and Career Ready (CCR) or Anchor Standards

These standards "anchor" the document and define general, cross-disciplinary literacy expectations. These are referred to as the *CCR Standards*. There are Anchor Standards for each strand. Anchor standards are the same for the entire section: K–5, 6–12, 6–12 Literacy.

## Grade-Level Specific Standards

Grade-Level Specific Standards define end-of-year expectations. They are a cumulative progression designed to enable students to meet college and career readiness by the end of high school. Students advancing through the grades are expected to meet each year's Grade-Level Standards, while working steadily toward meeting the more coherent expectations described by the CCR (Anchor) Standards. Each Grade-Level Standard is aligned to an Anchor Standard. The ELA CCSS strive to create and build:

- A focus on results rather than means

- An integrated model of literacy

- Research and media skills blended into the standards as a whole

- Shared responsibility for students' literacy development

- Focus and coherence in instruction and assessment

## Organization and Language of the Standards

Standards use the following terminology: Sections, Grade Levels, Grade Bands, Strands, and Numbers.

**Sections**—The ELA standards are grouped and organized into these sections: K–5 ELA; 6–12 ELA; and 6–12 Literacy in History, Social Studies, Science and Technical subjects.

**Grade Levels**—The standards are further organized by individual grade level (K–8).

**Grade Bands**—High School uses the grade bands of 9–10 and 11–12, which allows high schools flexibility in course design.

**English Language Arts (ELA) Strands**—Reading Literature; Reading Informational Text; Reading Foundational Skills; Writing; Speaking and Listening; Language; and Literacy in History, Social Studies, Science and Technical Subjects (Grades 6–12 only).

### How to Read the ELA Standards

**CCR Anchor Standards** can be identified by: Strand, CCR status, and Number (or number/letter). For example, **R.CCR.1** is an abbreviation of *Reading Strand, CCR Standard, Number 1*.

> R.CCR.1
> 1. Read closely to determine what the text says explicitly and to make logical inferences from it; cite specific textual evidence when writing or speaking to support conclusions drawn from the text.

**Grade-Level Specific Standards** can be identified by: Strand, Grade, Number. For example, **RI.3.1** abbreviates *Reading Informational Text, Grade 3, Number 1.*

> RI.3.1—Ask and answer questions to demonstrate understanding of a text, referring explicitly to the text as the basis for the answers.

## Anchor vs. Grade-Specific Standards

All Grade-Level Specific Standards align to an Anchor Standard (for example, Grade-Level RI.3.1 aligns with the Anchor R.CCR.1). Anchor Standards are broad skills and thinking processes that we want students to be able to do at the end of K–5 and then 6–12. There are six to ten Anchor Standards for each strand.

Grade-Specific Standards are the more discrete skills taught within each grade level that help to accomplish the overall goals of the Anchor Standards.

The CCR and Grade-Specific Standards are necessary complements— the former providing broad standards, the latter providing additional specificity—that together define the skills and understandings that all students should demonstrate.

## Breaking Down Anchor Standards and Grade-Specific Standards

To better understand these standards, we will break down an individual standard to determine what actions and thinking it is asking students to do.

First, let's take a closer look at a **Common Core Anchor Standard (CCR Standard):**

What is this Standard asking students to know or do?

> **R.CCR.1**
> 1. Read closely to determine what the text says explicitly and to make logical inferences from it; cite specific textual evidence when writing or speaking to support conclusions drawn from the text.

1. **Read** a piece of text and restate exactly what the text says. The first part of this Standard asks students to retrieve the information in front of them.

2. Make an **inference** from the text. To make an inference, the student needs to comprehend what he or she has just read by combining the text information with their own experiences and background knowledge about the subject.

3. Reason by **drawing a conclusion** about what the student read. This Standard asks students to retrieve right-there information, comprehend or understand what the text was about, and then to use reasoning skills to draw a conclusion.

Breaking down the standards reveals the details of what the Standard is asking students to do and the types of higher-order thinking it requires from students.

Let's take a closer look at a **Common Core Grade-Specific Standard**

RI.3.1—Ask and answer questions to demonstrate understanding of a text, referring explicitly to the text as the basis for the answers.

This third grade-specific standard requires students to understand what they have read by formulating questions and then proving they can be answered by using just the text provided. This means that students have to clearly read and pull information from complex text and understand it proficiently. This skill-based standard builds coherence in learning and helps students meet the anchor standard seen above.

## More Key Features of the ELA Common Core Standards

The Common Core ELA Standards were built around a portrait of what a college- and career-ready student should be able to demonstrate.

▶ Focus on broad thinking and communicating skills that students need for success

▶ Research and media skills are blended into the standards

▶ A shared responsibility for literacy development built in across the different academic disciplines

The Common Core defines that a literate individual:

- Demonstrates independence

- Builds strong content knowledge

- Responds to the varying demands of audience, task, purpose and discipline

- Comprehends as well as critiques

- Values evidence

- Uses technology and digital media strategically and capably

- Comes to understand other perspectives and cultures

The Common Core is designed so that as students advance through the grades and master the standards in reading, writing, speaking, listening, and language, they will exhibit with increasing fullness and regularity the capacities of the literate individual as defined above.

## 21st Century Design and Delivery with the Common Core

21st century instructional design and delivery is not just about using technology, it involves much more. It is about understanding the collision of new, more rigorous standards, embedded 21st century skills, authentic tasks, multiple learning pathways, performance assessments, and understanding how to leverage technology to make all of this happen. Online performance-based assessments are being developed to align with the CCSS. These new assessments will replace our current annual state assessments and will be used to evaluate individual student progress and school and district growth and achievement benchmarks. We will go more in-depth about these assessments in Chapter 4.

# Common Core State Standards: Mathematics

The Common Core State Standards in Mathematics (CCSSM) also seek to create a shift in our thinking around teaching, learning, and the purpose of math instruction. Key changes in the math standards include:

▶ Coherency across grade spans

▶ Focused teaching: depth not breadth to reach rigor

▶ Application and purpose of mathematics in life

Let's look at the language of how the Common Core Mathematics Standards are organized and then we will revisit how these changes listed above affect learning for students and how we will teach mathematics.

CCSSM also consist of two types of standards: Standards for **Mathematical Practice** and Standards for **Mathematical Content**.

## Standards for Mathematical Practice

The Standards for **Mathematical Practice** are the bigger picture mathematical skills and thinking processes that we want all students to be able to do. They are the same for all grades and are the cumulative goal of the Common Core Math Standards (like the ELA CCR or Anchor Standards).

The Common Core Standards for Mathematical Practice "describe varieties of expertise that mathematics educators at all levels should seek to develop in their students. These practices rest on important 'processes and proficiencies' with long-standing importance in mathematics education," (2010). The Standards for Mathematical Practice expect a student to be able to:

▶ Make sense of problems and persevere in solving them

▶ Reason abstractly and quantitatively

▶ Attend to precision

▶ Look for and make use of structure

▶ Construct viable arguments and critique the reasoning of others

▶ Model with mathematics

▶ Use appropriate tools strategically

▶ Look for and express regularity in repeated reasoning

These skills profile the mathematical thinking that the Common Core seeks for all students.

## Standards for Mathematical Content

The Standards for Mathematical Content are a combination of procedure and understanding statements. The Common Core seeks to create understanding of mathematical *concepts and the procedural skills* necessary for successful mathematical reasoning and for all students to be college- and career-ready.

Conceptual understanding and skill mastery go hand-in-hand and are essential to creating students who can compete in a global society. Designers of mathematics instructional materials, assessments, and professional development should all aim to connect mathematical practices to mathematical content.

## How to Read Mathematical Content Standards

The Content Standards are organized by Grade Level, Domain, Cluster, and Standard.

▶ **Domains** are larger groups of related standards. Standards from different domains may sometimes be closely related

▶ **Cluster Standards** summarize groups of related standards. Because mathematics is a connected subject, *standards* from different *clusters* are sometimes closely related.

▶ **Standards** define what students should understand and be able to do

| SAMPLE (Kindergarten): | |
|---|---|
| **Domain** | Counting and Cardinality<br>K.CC .1 |
| **Standard** | Know number names and the count sequence. |
| **Cluster** | Count to 100 by ones and tens.<br>Count forward beginning from a given number with the known sequence (instead of having to begin at 1).<br>Write numbers from 0 to 20. Represent a number of objects with a written numeral 0-20 (with 0 representing a count of no objects). |

The **Domains** vary across the grade levels with increasing complexity.

| Domains: Grades K–8 | |
|---|---|
| **Grade K** | Counting and Cardinality (K.CC)<br>Operations and Algebraic Thinking (K.OA)<br>Number Operations in Base Ten (K.NBT)<br>Measurement and Data (K.MD)<br>Geometry (K.G) |
| **Grades 1–2** | Operations and Algebraic Thinking (1.OA or 2.OA)<br>Number Operations in Base Ten (1.NBT or 2.NBT)<br>Measurement and Data (1.MD or 2.MD)<br>Geometry (1.G or 2.G) |
| **Grades 3–5** | Operations and Algebraic Thinking (3.OA or 4.OA or 5.OA)<br>Number Operations in Base Ten (3.NBT or 4.NBT or 5.NBT)<br>Number Operations – Fractions (3.NF or 4.NF or 5.NF)<br>Measurement and Data (3.MD or 4.MD or 5.MD)<br>Geometry (3.G or 4.G or 5.G) |
| **Grades 6–7** | Ratios and Proportional Relationships (6.RP or 7.RP)<br>The Number System (6.NS or 7.NS)<br>Expressions and Equations (6.EE or 7.EE)<br>Geometry (6.G or 7.G)<br>Statistics and Probability (6.SP or 7.SP) |
| **Grade 8** | The Number System (8.NS )<br>Expressions and Equations (8.EE)<br>Functions (8.F)<br>Geometry (8.G)<br>Statistics and Probability (8.SP) |

The number of **standards** and **cluster standards** within each domain varies within each grade level. Often cluster standards may overlap across grade levels and build in complexity as math concepts are connected through the grade level progression. The cluster standards are numbered under each Standard.

The Math CCSS do not indicate the order in which concepts need to be taught, giving teachers room to design their own classroom instruction from within the standards. The CCSS documents explain this as follows:

> *...just because topic A appears before topic B in the standards for a given grade, it does not necessarily mean that topic A must be taught before topic B. A teacher might prefer to teach topic B before topic A, or might choose to highlight connections by teaching topic A and topic B at the same time. Or, a teacher might prefer to teach a topic of his or her own choosing that leads, as a byproduct, to students reaching the standards for topic A and B. (CCSS 2010)*

The CCSS seek to **focus** instructional designers—the teacher—on the *connectedness* of concepts and content. In reading the domains above, you can see how the content of the domains builds both conceptual and procedural knowledge of mathematics all the way through the grades K–8.

**High school math is organized into the following Content Areas:**

- Number and Quantity Overview
- Algebra Overview
- High School Functions
- High School Modeling
- Geometry Overview
- High School Statistics and Probability

Within each of those content areas are varied content specific domains, standards, and cluster standards. *(We will not list them all here but they can be referenced in the CCSS documents.)*

It will be interesting to see how CCSS in Mathematics affects high school course offerings and content organization at that level. High school content is specifically not labeled by grade level to allow for flexibility within the system. States traditionally have done a variety of things with math offerings and progression and the CCSS provides states the opportunity to continue to do so as well as providing guidance for intent around these choices. Algebraic concepts are built beginning in kindergarten, the full course content is placed at the high school level.

Although the trend for the past decade has been to have all students through algebra by eighth grade, many feel that students are not developmentally ready for algebra at that age. Although CCSS lists this as high school content, it does not indicate anywhere that accelerated courses are not recommended nor does it recommend them in any way at this time. We believe that all content, grade level assignment and acceleration considerations should be based on individual student needs. We will address this further in Chapter 6— Customizing and Enriching Student Learning.

## Key Changes in Math Standards: Focus-Coherency-Application

CCSS seeks to create connections for students across their mathematical career. It provides new ways for students to apply and use the math foundations they have from elementary and middle school when they reach high school. CCSS for high school math embeds modeling and real life application across all content areas in all standards and courses. The goal has shifted from getting through math content and memorizing multiple procedures, to applying the math to understand the world around us. Most state standards tended to chunk math skills. Skills were often organized in isolation which created a feeling of disconnectedness to students.

Math *is* connected to everything. The CCSS progression from kindergarten to high school graduation seeks to highlight and build these connections to create citizens who can use math to understand the world around them. They are also intended to help students problem solve in their daily lives and careers. The CCSS developers studied the teaching and organization of learning mathematics in countries where math achievement rates were among the highest. They used this information to guide the development of CCSSM in hopes to create a society that can compete in all areas including the mathematical needs of our global economy.

Focus, coherency, connections, and application will now guide our design and delivery choices as we implement the Common Core in Mathematics.

## Standards Familiarity is Foundational

Spend time getting to know your state standards in all subjects that you are responsible for teaching. Get to know their design and intent and become familiar with the language and organization of your standards. This will provide good dialogue and collaboration options when speaking with colleagues about the standards. Then dig in and look for the student thinking embedded in the standards. This is where instructional design begins.

# Reaching Beyond the Standards

As you go through the instructional design process you will be making choices about the activities, experiences, and tasks that students will engage in while learning each Standard. As you choose and build their learning through experiences, you have the opportunity to vary the Cognitive Growth Targets that students will use and you can intentionally reach higher level thinking skills. Always keep in mind that you are not limited by the cognitive targets embedded in the standards. You are the architect and you are using the standards to build thinking for your students—there's no limit on "how" you choose to foster higher-order thinking in your classroom.

In later chapters, as you build unit and lesson plans, you will have the opportunity to align student engagement choices with the Cognitive Growth Targets and 21st Century Skills.

## Blueprint Essentials

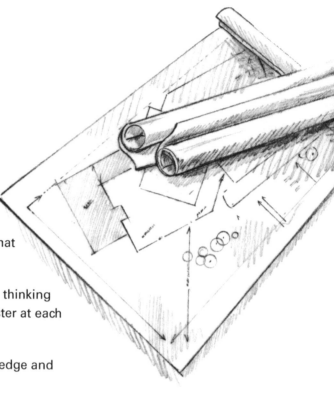

Know and understand your
state's standards for all subjects that
you teach.

Standards embed knowledge and thinking
that students are expected to master at each
grade level.

Analyze your standards for knowledge and
higher-order thinking.

Opportunities to freelance in your classroom exist in the gaps
you see in the Standards.

The gap between design and teaching in the classroom is closed
by identifying actions that support your state and local standards.

Leveraging technology to design, deliver, and assess student learning
is essential to teaching  21st century skills and Common Core rigor.

## Reflection and Action

▶ Obtain a copy of your state standards for each content area you teach. Remember, some content areas may not have state standards. This can vary from state to state.

▶ Locate any additional school or district standards you are expected to teach. Begin by asking your principal or visiting your school or district website. You could also reach out to other grade level teachers for additional resources and support.

▶ Perform an initial analysis of the thinking and 21st century skills associated with your state standards.

▶ What are your initial thoughts about thinking as it relates to your standards? How do they line up with your definition of higher-order thinking? How can you use this information to design experiences for your students?

## In the Library

**The Common Core State Standards:
http://www.corestandards.org**

*Understanding Common Core Standards* (2011)
John Kendall

*Something in Common: The Common Core State Standards and the Next Chapter in American Education* (2011)
Robert Rothman

*Navigating the Common Core Handbook Series* (2011)
The Leadership and Learning Center

# Journal Entry

**Experiencing and Personalizing your Journey**

**Enjoyment List**: Write down 20 things you enjoy about teaching. Teaching provides many intrinsic rewards, even in the midst of the obstacles and challenges you face every day. Revisit this list throughout your journey as a reminder.

**Inspiration:** Think of a time when one of your students or a student's parent took the time to say thank you or gave you a compliment. It might have been spoken or through email or a hand-written note. Whatever the case, it probably inspired you to do more and it made you feel good about how much you've done for your students. If you still have the note (or email) consider attaching it here or create a larger scrapbook of all your thank you notes. If the thank you or compliment was verbal, take the time to write it down. These small but powerful inspirational moments are important reminders of why you are in this work.

# Chapter 4

# Are My Students Learning?

## The Power of Assessments

## A Teacher's Story: Are My Students Learning?

*"I taught Spot to fetch."*

*"I said I taught him. I didn't say he learned it."*

## Connect and Reflect

Anyone who has ever taught has probably felt like this at one time or another. While humorous in this cartoon, there is a serious gap between teaching and learning that is bridged only by the power of purposeful assessment.

A culture determines which skills and knowledge are necessary for students to contribute, and asks teachers and schools to manage that information. We understand historically what our American democracy has asked of public education and know that our time now is no different.

Outlining the academic journey that a culture has prescribed for students is a process teachers take on every day. You are familiar with planning out your students' learning and have questioned: "What should my students know and be able to do?" You have pondered critical learning and higher-order thinking—from the perspective of your own experience, views from your community and state, our common America, and those of the global society. Now we move on to the proof of your planning—assessments.

**Assessment,** the proof of a good build, is a necessary and vital part of the design of high-quality classroom instruction, and we cannot understate assessment's merit and value.

To make assessment truly useful, begin by determining your purpose and intent and then contemplate what evidence you want to collect to determine if students have:

a) demonstrated mastery of the desired knowledge and concepts, and

b) the ability to perform a task with this new knowledge. In other words: Do you have proof that your students learned what was intended?

*Considering what evidence is necessary to determine that your students are in fact meeting desired or required objectives is a recent practice in education.*

## Why We Do What We Do

Begin first by determining your **purpose and intent** for assessment. Are you looking for information about your students so you can plan instruction that is academically appropriate or are you looking for information about whether or not your students learned content you just taught? Both are important for different reasons. When thinking about designing an assessment strategy in your own classroom you will want to consider four specific purposes: universal screening, diagnostics, progress monitoring, and summative assessments. Sometimes assessments may be used for more than one purpose.

*As our journey continues, ponder the different outcomes of two small words in the same phrase:*

*Teaching **and** learning*

*Teaching **for** learning*

**Universal screening** allows teachers to quickly understand students' general deficiencies. Screening assessments quickly identify if a student has general deficits measured against a pre-determined benchmark, typically by month or quarter and grade level.

**Diagnostics** allow teachers to diagnose students' specific needs. Diagnostic measures tend to break down general measures into specific skills and strategies. For instance, a screening assessment may alert a teacher to a particular child's "phonics" deficiency while a diagnostic assessment may indicate the child's specific "diphthongs and digraphs" weakness.

**Progress monitoring** allows teachers to monitor progress in addressing the specific needs. Progress monitoring assessments are administered once instruction has begun and provide teachers with information concerning *how* students are responding to the targeted instruction. Typically, the progress monitoring assessments are in direct correlation to what was taught and help teachers monitor and adjust future instruction. These assessments help teachers answer the question: *Have my students learned what I just taught?* There are both formal and informal progress monitoring assessments and they vary in frequency and duration.

**Summative assessments** are not limiting and allow teachers to have a summary of the learning over a particular period of time. There are many types of summative assessments and may occur at the end of a unit of study, a course, or a school year.

| Determining Purpose and Intent | | |
|---|---|---|
| **Measuring Growth Over Time** | Does my school have a universal assessment that adapts for individual students in reading and math at least three times per year? Is the scale independent of grade level? How will I measure learning in other subjects like science, social studies and the arts? | |
| **Demonstrating End-Of-Unit Understanding** | After creating my units of study (usually between 4–8 per year) do I have end-of-unit assessments that ask students for selected and constructed responses? Are these assessments aligned to state standards? College readiness standards? End-of-year goals? Do I have performance assessments at the end of the units of study? How will I ask students to demonstrate their deep understanding of content through performance? How will I know if learning has transferred? | Given time constraints, it may be difficult to incorporate lengthy project or performance-based assessments for every unit. The key is to have multiple opportunities for students across the school year. |
| **Monitoring Weekly and Daily Learning** | Do I have informal checks for understanding built-in on a weekly or daily basis? Do I use a combination of ways to collect this evidence? Exit tickets? Observations? Student conferences? | |

## Types of Assessments: Collect Evidence

High-quality instructional design includes all types of methods for collecting evidence of student learning and each are useful for developing students that are thinkers, problem-solvers, and creators. As architects of instruction, teachers can design and collect many methods of evidence of student learning from a continuum of assessments that varies in **time** (single lesson to end of unit); **rigor** (retrieve knowledge to create original products); and **context** (decontextualized to real-world relevance).

- ▶ Informal Checks for Understanding
- ▶ Constructed Response
- ▶ Selected Response

- ▶ Conferences
- ▶ Observations
- ▶ Performance Tasks

### Informal Checks for Understanding

**Informal checks** for understanding happen most during a single lesson. Typically, teachers can provide several opportunities for students to demonstrate knowledge of the lesson, for instance by using teacher questioning, student-to-student dialogue, and student work. As teachers, we can respond to student misunderstanding or misconceptions by providing additional modeling or inquiry as they work with new knowledge or concepts.

*Informal checks for understanding happen throughout the lesson, typically during guided or independent practice, or at the end of a lesson as well.*

*Exit tickets are a common way to collect informal evidence.*

Although there are several ways great teachers check for student understanding, one of the most important elements is *how* these teachers do it. The most effective teachers center their questions on the big ideas and concepts of their lesson. They plan for the situations in which they will invoke their students' understanding of the current lesson. For effective teachers, these situations:

▶ Are strategic

▶ Are pre-planned

▶ Involve checking for all students in the class

▶ Have a systemic way to record the information

▶ Use the information to understand student misconceptions by probing deeper with students (requiring active listening on the part of the teacher)

▶ Use student responses and misunderstanding as a teaching moment so that student misconceptions can be addressed in real-time

▶ Return swiftly to the lesson, because pacing and productivity matter

## Observations

Observation occurs during the lesson, when a teacher makes verbal or written notes of students who are working with the knowledge or concept. Whiteboards, student responses, and practice tasks are all vehicles for teachers to record observations and collect evidence.

## Conferences

Individual or small group student conferences in which students do most of the talking can happen while the rest of the class is working independently. Students are asked to explain their thinking about a particular topic or concept, or defend a position using evidence from a text or personal experience. Questions during conferences should address a range of inquiry, from remembering and understanding to more complex questions that judge a student's analysis and synthesis of the information.

## Selected Response

Selected response assessments are probably the most familiar to teachers. In this assessment, students must choose an answer from a limited set of possibilities, such as multiple choice, matching, or true/false. Typically, these assessments are best known for having "one right answer." They are most helpful to determine if students have remembered or understood declarative, procedural, or conceptual knowledge.

## Absolute vs. Adaptive Selected Response

While there are several selected response assessments, the most common is multiple choice. Multiple choice assessments fall in two design categories: absolute and adaptive. **Absolute multiple choice** assessments are typically written at a specific grade level or standard. They assess student mastery of content and knowledge and provide evidence for teachers on how students are learning isolated, discrete skills within a unit, semester, or year.

In contrast, **adaptive multiple choice** tests do not assess student mastery but rather provide evidence of a larger continuum of learning and mark student growth over time. They challenge assumptions about grade level performance because they are dynamic and adapt in real time as students select their answers. Typically, there is one scale, broken down into equal intervals and are independent of student grade level. The assessment can provide useful information about the student's instructional level and evidence of growth in the set of discrete skills.

## Constructed Response

Constructed response assessments are used when a teacher wants a student to produce a short or extended response to a specific prompt or explain their rationale and thinking about a particular topic or procedural task. Often, this assessment is scored using a rubric developed against a pre-determined set of criteria. Typically, there is no "one right answer" but rather students must use their own language and decisions and apply, synthesize, evaluate, or analyze specific knowledge to answer the question.

## Performance-Based Assessments

Performance assessments require students to produce original work from specific learning outcomes and are most often used to culminate a unit of study. The creation of these projects or performances require students to reason through a complex set of challenges, much like problems of the real world. Typically, these performances or projects are authentic in nature and can involve knowledge across several academic and arts-related domains. Often, there is an audience for the performance or project, and if the project was created over a longer period of time, both the process and product are assessed.

However, performance assessments take on many forms, and do not always need to be project-based. Daily or weekly performance assessments can be an active part of a classroom assessment strategy. Typically, these types of performance assessments often involve student writing. Authentic writing tasks, where students produce original work spread over a myriad of writing genres, can be a powerful way to assess student learning.

# Reliability and Validity in Assessment

As the architect of your classroom's learning, you want to ensure that how you are measuring student learning aligns with what you want your students to learn. How do you evaluate your assessments for quality?

How do you make sure your assessments are valid *and* reliable?

**Validity** refers to our ability to generalize about results, or our confidence in knowing that what we are asking students to demonstrate accurately reflects what they know and can do. In contrast, **reliability** refers to the consistency of our measurement and the degree to which our assessments are the same each time we use them.

## Selected Response Assessment Validity and Reliability

▶ When evaluating items on a selected response assessment, one thing to consider is how the question is asked.

▶ Does the question represent all the types of declarative, procedural, and conceptual knowledge you want students to know?

▶ Are there other ways to ask the same question?

▶ What is the degree of difficulty of the question?
Which *Cognitive Growth Targets* does the question align to?

▶ Can it be solved in one step or several?

▶ Does the question simply ask students to recall a specific procedure or must they apply it in another context?

## Rubrics

One of the most common ways to assess student learning is by using **rubrics.** Although rubrics are powerful assessment measures of student learning, building valid and reliable rubrics can be complex and challenging. A well written rubric communicates what is expected of an assignment and thus provides a means to evaluate each student's work.

## Recordkeeping

In our fieldwork with schools, we have found that the most effective teachers are never surprised by results because they had a method for recording assessment results all along the way. Recordkeeping not only happened with formal grading, end-of-unit assessments, and weekly quizzes, but also *within the moment* assessments and daily checks for understanding.

*One of the best ways we have found to build a valid and reliable **RUBRIC** is to begin by examining student work.*

*Sort the work into developmental stages, usually making four or five piles of work that span the proficiency continuum.*

*Generalize and describe each pile of work, writing down specific traits from each group.*

*Once this is complete, you can begin to build a rubric that measures the degree of proficiency for the performance or project.*

*You will continuously refine the rubric as you score student responses. Over time, if your rubric reflects the desired understanding and critical learning you want your students to know and be able to do—and if the scores on the rubric are consistent over the years—then it's safe to conclude that the rubric you built is both valid and reliable.*

We have seen recordkeeping in many different forms, and although highly-effective teachers' methods for recordkeeping spanned the assessment continuum, whatever form it took, it was always present during instruction. Graphs, charts, numeric values, quick notes, and longer descriptive analysis are just some of the methods we have seen successful teachers use. However, each of these recordkeeping methods was tightly-aligned to the objectives that students were asked to master. The recordkeeping accurately noted the extent to which each student was progressing towards mastery of the objectives.

## Guiding Questions

▶ Which assessments do you use in your classroom today?

▶ What types of assessments are they?

▶ What assessments are mandated by your state? Your district? Your school?

▶ What assessments do or will you create on your own?

▶ How do you think about assessment alignment?

▶ If students were successful on your classroom assessments, what would they know and be able to do?

## Connecting to Classroom Practice

A New Era Begins: Standards

At the time of publication of this book, our nation is embarking on a new set of learning standards for students. As you read in Chapter 3, the Common Core State Standards were designed to increase the rate at which students graduate from high school, college, and become career-ready. This goal requires a massive overhaul of individual state's assessment systems, and two new assessment systems have been selected for this purpose. Nearly half of the states have chosen to join the **Partnership for Assessment of Readiness for College and Careers (PARCC),** while the other half have joined **Smarter Balanced Assessment Consortium (SMARTER Balanced).**

A few states have chosen to keep their current state standards by not adopting the Common Core State Standards. Check to see if your state adopted the new Common Core.

For those of you in PARCC states, your new state assessment will be a series of summative assessments given across the school year. For English Language Arts, students will take four Through-Course assessments and one End-of-Year Comprehensive Assessment. In mathematics, students will take three Through-Course assessments and one End-of-Year Comprehensive Assessment. The following section details the new requirements.

## PARCC Through-Course and End-Of-Year Comprehensive Assessments

### PARCC English Language Arts (ELA)

At the end of approximately the first and second quarter, students take Through-Course Assessment 1 and 2. Each assessment will be completed in a single session and involve one or two focused literacy tasks in which students read a selected text, draw evidence from it, form conclusions, and write an analysis.

At the end of the third quarter, students take Through-Course Assessment 3 and 4. They are completed over several sessions or class periods, and students are asked to complete a longer written task in which they conduct electronic searches (from pre-defined digital sources), evaluate the authenticity and quality of the sources, and then write an essay or research paper. The digital sources will represent a range of text levels at each grade level. The fourth Through-Course assessment is required, but not used for accountability purposes. In this assessment, students present their written work from Assessment 3 to their classmates. Teachers score the student's listening and speaking skills using a standardized rubric. This score may be used for grading purposes, but it will not be used for state accountability purposes.

Finally, there will be an End-of Year (EOY) assessment, composed of 40–65 questions representing a range of complexity, and will be taken online during the last few weeks of school.

## PARCC Mathematics

In mathematics, students will take three Through-Course assessments and one End-of-Year Assessment. The first and second Through-Course assessments will be taken at the end of the first and second quarters. The assessments will largely focus on essential topics within the Common Core State Standards. The third Through-Course assessment will be given at the end of the third quarter and require students to apply mathematical skills (key concepts and processes) to multistep problems. For instance, students will be expected to use technological tools to graph functions, create bar graphs, and draw lines of symmetry. Finally, an End-of-Year (EYO) assessment will be given online, similar to the ELA assessment.

## SMARTER Balanced Summative Assessments

If you are a teacher in states that have adopted the **SMARTER** Balanced assessment system, all students in grades 3–8 and high school will be given mandatory summative assessments administered in the last 12 weeks of the school year. These summative assessments are given in English Language Arts and Mathematics and include a combination of computer-adaptive assessments and performance tasks.

## Interim Assessments

Optional interim assessments are available to schools and districts; they are designed as item sets that cluster standards based upon content. Your school or district will be able to administer these assessments at strategic points during the school year. The interim assessments include adaptive assessments, constructed response assessments, and performance assessments.

## Scoring and Accountability

At the time of printing, both PARCC and Smarter Balanced consortiums are still developing their scoring and accountability.

# Building Your Classroom Assessment Strategy

The first step in planning your own classroom assessment strategy is to identify what assessments your school, district, and state mandate and/or have available to you. Next, understand with clarity the purpose and intent of each those assessments.

**Record this information here:**

| | Assessment Name | Purpose | | | | Type of Assessment | | | | | |
|---|---|---|---|---|---|---|---|---|---|---|---|
| | | Universal Screening | Diagnostic | Progress Monitoring | Summative | Informal Check | Observation | Conferences | Selected Response | Constructed Responses | Performance Assessment |
| **State Mandated** | | | | | | | | | | | |
| **District Mandated** | | | | | | | | | | | |
| **School Mandated** | | | | | | | | | | | |

Ask these questions to think about what types of classroom assessments you need to add to balance your current documentation:

▶ Do these assessments move across the continuum and provide a rich array of opportunities for my students to demonstrate knowledge on many levels?

▶ Does my school or district offer optional assessments that might be worth considering?

Study the content and questioning of each assessment. Use the Cognitive Growth Targets to determine if your assessments provide evidence that students are demonstrating all levels of cognitive complexity.

Once you have identified and evaluated the mandated assessments, begin creating an **instructional calendar** that documents specific student assessment dates throughout the school year. This calendar will evolve as you continue the journey through this book.

Once you have considered the chart, add the anticipated assessment dates to your instructional calendar. Remember, your instructional calendar is an evolving document.

## Sample Instructional Calendar

| First Semester | August | | September | | | | October | | |
|---|---|---|---|---|---|---|---|---|---|
| Week | 1 | 2 | 3 | 4 | 5 | 6 | 7 | 8 | 9 |
| Fall Adaptive Assessment | | | | | | | | | |
| District Reading Assessments | | | | | | | | | |
| State Assessments | | | | | | | Fall PARCC | | |
| Progress Reports and Grading Periods | | | | Progress Reports | | | | | Report Cards |
| Staff Meetings | | | | | | | | | |
| Instructional Leadership Team Meetings (ILT) | | | | | | | | | |
| Grade Level Teacher Team Meetings (TT) | | | | | | | | | |

We often see school systems over-assessing students—remember to be clear about the intent of each assessment. There is no need to create an assessment if you are already giving a similar assessment required by your school, district, or state. For example, if your school requires you to give a literacy assessment every four weeks that is connected to a specific reading program your school uses, you may not need to have an end-of-unit selected or constructed response assessment. However, this may be the time to create a performance assessment to confirm higher-level understanding if the built-in reading program assessments do not ask students to demonstrate their understanding in that manner. Be intentional and purposeful when selecting, creating, and administering assessments.

## Blueprint Essentials

There are several different types of educational assessments. Selected and constructed responses are two of the most popular.

Performance assessments extend student thinking by requiring the learner to create and produce authentic, original work. These assessments often involve the application of isolated discrete skills into a coherent whole and can sometimes require the integration of content areas and interdisciplinary knowledge.

Classroom teachers should develop an instructional calendar that maps out an assessment schedule as well as the types of assessments students will be required to take over the course of a school year.

Connected to and aligned with the classroom instructional calendar should be a systemic way the classroom teacher records and disseminates assessment data with students and parents.

## In the Library

### Assessment

*Introduction to Student-Involved Assessment FOR Learning (6th Edition)* (2011)
Rick J. Stiggins, Jan Chappuis

*Classroom Assessment for Student Learning: Doing It Right - Using It Well* (2004)
Richard J. Stiggins, Judith A. Arter, Jan Chappuis, Stephen Chappuis

# Reflection and Action

## Reflection

▶ How aligned are your assessments with your state standards? Can you match assessments questions with your state standards?

▶ Which types of assessments lend themselves towards higher-order thinking?

▶ Do some of your assessments ask students to reason or create?

▶ Do you agree or disagree with anything you've read in this chapter? How does your experience support your opinion?

▶ What would you do differently after reading this chapter?

▶ Which of your practices have been affirmed?

▶ Which state assessments do you believe advance individual classroom goals?

## Action

▶ Collect all of the assessments you plan to give this school year.

▶ Begin building your classroom assessment strategy.

▶ Begin creating your instructional calendar.

▶ Use the Cognitive Growth Targets to perform an initial analysis of your assessments.

# Journal Entry

**Experiencing and
Personalizing your Journey**

**Letter Writing:** When is the last time you took the time to write a letter to someone long-hand? In today's digital age letter writing has become a lost art. Take the time to write an encouraging letter to yourself about your teaching practice in the space here.

Compliment yourself for what you do well. Include items from the enjoyment list in Chapter 3 to round out the encouragement letter. If you wrote your letter on a separate piece of paper, attach the letter here.

# Chapter 5

# Brain Storm:
## Four Colliding Forces

# A Teacher's Story: Memory

*When I was 23, I spent a month traveling with two friends around Europe: seven countries, seven different languages. We were just three of the thousands in the backpacker circuit. I remember that time vividly but there is one memory that, over a decade later, still sticks with me.*

*We'd just finished three exciting days in Paris and arrived early at Gare du Nord to anxiously await our next destination: Munich. The Parisian train station, built in 1846, is beautiful, massive in its demeanor yet gracious in the way it handles its travelers. It was easy to spot the American backpackers and Gare du Nord had its fair share that evening.*

*We didn't have a lot of money, so cutting expenses was a large part of the experience. We often ate bread and cheese to avoid pricey restaurants and although we rode the Euro rail at night so we didn't have to pay for hotels, the sleeper cars were too expensive.*

*Since most trains opened their doors an hour before departure, we thought we had enough time to find a comfortable spot to sleep on the train— a quad of seats facing each other. The last train out was scheduled at 10:30 pm. But as we approached the ticket counter at 9:30, we noticed blinking lights—a last boarding call for Munich. And in bewilderment, we watched as the last train pulled out of the station. The next train wasn't scheduled until 6:30 the next morning.*

*So we did what any experienced backpacker would do: we slept in the train station that night. We set up camp, about 25 feet from the rail, using our backpacks as pillows, and settled in for the evening. Throughout the night, the smell of the rail at Gare du Nord crept into my head. It was distinct and had an unforgettable complexity to it. And the metal had a patina to it not unlike that of the many steel factories inhabiting the Midwest rustbelt.*

*I live in Chicago now and often ride our elevated, or "El" train system throughout the city. There are certain times while waiting for the train that the smell of the rail will bring back that memory of our night at the Gare du Nord. It happens without thought. The smell, then the flashback: three of us sleeping on the ground, backpacks as pillows, waiting for the morning train to Germany. I remember, distinctly, even the clothes I was wearing: khaki shorts, a green and white polo shirt. It was truly a night I will never forget.*

## Connect and Reflect

Surely, many of you have memories like this. Maybe the smell of your grandmother's cooking, or fresh cut grass after your father finished mowing the lawn, salty air from a family vacation—whatever the memory, why do certain experiences stay with us forever and how are those memories formed? Why is it not as easy to recall the Periodic Table in chemistry class as it was to remember the details of that night in Paris?

How does the brain store permanent information into our memories— and how do we recall those memories when we want or need to? How does the human brain process, store, and retrieve information? And what implications do these questions have for me as a teacher? We explore answers to these questions as our journey continues.

## Why We Do What We Do

The human brain is the most complex natural system in the universe. Some have labeled it science's new frontier (Goldberg, 2001, p.23). Scientists are learning about the brain at an exponential rate, giving us greater opportunity to know even more about the human mind. We believe that the construction of the mind from the activity generated by the brain should also be education's new frontier.

Yet for most of us, teacher preparation programs might have had a few classes on learning theory but none on brain research. The stark reality is that higher education and education policy makers have been reluctant to move too swiftly into brain research and its implications for informing learning theories and teacher practice (Organisation for Economic Co-operation and Development, 2002, p.69).

*Fortunately, the accountability movement shifted researcher and practitioner focus from studying a teacher's content knowledge and teaching methods to students' learning and the effectiveness of teaching methods on students' ability to learn the content. This new focus has led to more sophisticated research methods— often applied in other sciences— when studying the effects of pedagogy on student learning.*

As cognitive neuroscience evolves, so do methodologies for studying how children process, store, and retrieve information, giving the teaching profession great hope about our ability to scientifically and creatively design instruction that considers individual student strengths and weaknesses within cultural and social contexts.

We've observed and concluded that our most successful teachers have a command of the learning theories and use them to inform their instructional design. There have been hundreds of books written about learning theories. This chapter is meant to give you a basic overview of some of the most fundamental concepts on learning theory and its implications for instructional design.

## The Human Brain

While each brain has minor "folds" that are unique to each individual, all human brains share some common characteristics. The outer structure of the brain is divided into four major lobes, which in turn have three major internal parts: the brain stem, cerebrum, and limbic system. Each lobe is responsible for different executive functions of the brain.

The **frontal lobe** is primarily responsible for intellectual thinking such as abstract thought, decision making, and future planning, in addition to behavioral functions, voluntary movement, speech, and Broca's area, which is important in language production.

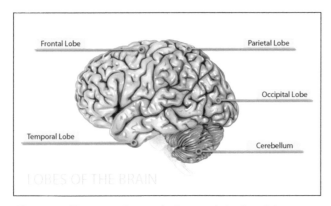

*Figure 5.1* illustrates the cerebellum and the four lobes of the brain

The **temporal lobe** controls auditory functions such as sound and speech and selected parts of long-term memory associated with visual memory, like face recognition on the right side of the temporal lobe. The left side aids in verbal memory so humans can understand and remember language. The rear of the lobe assists in interpreting other people's emotions and reactions.

The **parietal lobe** interprets many of the inputs received in the brain and processed in other lobes. The parietal lobe helps us make meaning from these inputs, including spatial and temporal reasoning, sensation, orientation, and recognition.

The **occipital lobes** are the visual processing center of the brain. They are the smallest of four paired lobes in the human cerebral cortex and are found in the very back of the skull.

*Figure 5.2* is a diagram of the inner brain and identifies the cerebrum, amygdala, hippocampus, thalamus, and the brain stem

The **cerebellum,** sometimes referred to as the "little brain," is primarily responsible for motor functions. The cerebellum, however, is responsible for some cognitive functions such as attention and language.

When we look inside the outer structures of the brain we find three parts: the brain stem, cerebrum, and limbic system. Each one is responsible for its own general functions.

The **brain stem** controls many of the automatic functions of the brain that we don't have to think about: heartbeat, body temperature, respiration, digestion. The brain stem houses the reticular activating system (RAS), which controls the brain's alertness.

The **cerebrum** is divided into the left and right hemispheres and is often what people refer to when discussing the *brain*.

The **limbic system** controls most of the emotions we feel and is divided into three parts: the thalamus, amygdala, and hippocampus, each controlling parts of the processing of information.

▶ **Thalamus:** incoming sensory information comes into the brain through the thalamus (except smell, which we will explain further later) and then directed to other parts of the brain for further processing.

▶ **Amygdala:** the Greek word for *almond* because of its shape, the amygdala is primarily responsible for emotion, especially fear. The amygdala encodes emotions just before information is tagged for long-term memory. This is why when many people recall memories that were emotional to them, they re-live that emotion.

▶ **Hippocampus:** the Greek word for seahorse because of its shape, the hippocampus transmits information from working memory to long-term memory and storage. It is constantly trying to make meaning from new information coming into the brain through our senses and checking the information with information that is already stored (prior knowledge and past experiences).

The inner structures of the brain are made up of trillions of cells. There are two types of known cells: neurons and glial cells. **Neurons** are the basic functional unit of the nervous system. **Glial cells** provide support and nutrients for the neurons (*glial* is the Greek word for *glue*).

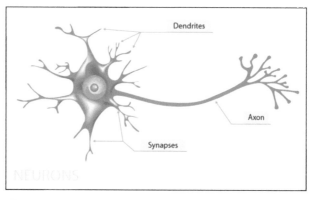

**Figure 5.3** *illustrates the relationship between the synapses, dendrites, and axons in a neuron.*

Neurons do not connect with each other but instead communicate by way of axons, dendrites, and synapses. These actions inside the cells are electrical while the actions between the cells are chemical. The electrical actions travel along the neurons.

▶ **Axons** send information from one neuron to another.

▶ **Dendrites** receive the information from the axons. Greek word for *tree*.

▶ **Synapses** are the tiny gaps that exist between and join axons and dendrites. Greek word for *joining together*.

Understanding the basic structure of the brain and the regions responsible for particular functions enhances understanding of the theories on how the brain learns.

## How the Brain Learns

Several years ago I was an adjunct professor at Chapman University. During my time there, I had the privilege of team teaching the graduate course *Discover Learning in the Mind, Brain, and Body* with UCLA neuroscientist, Dr. Teena Moody. Later, we wrote about our experience. The following excerpt appeared in *Chapman University Magazine.*

*When students are taught the behavioral aspects of learning theory they can also link those ideas to how knowledge is organized in the brain and what parts of the brain are activated during different activities. Hands-on experiences—actually touching the parts of the brain responsible for language, sight, touch, memory, self-control—can remind teachers that each child is unique and that the learning modality that works best for one child will not work for another.*

*Watching the initial reactions of students when they first see a human brain is fascinating. Disbelief is first for many, "Is it really a human brain?" Wonder and sometimes worry follow: "I didn't think it would look like that!" "Whose is it?" "Is it still alive?" (Some students watch too many bad science-fiction films.) We wear gloves to examine the brains, and while the smell of preservatives pushes some students to the edges of the classroom, we encourage all students to touch the brains, to feel the smoothness, and to follow the contours of the sulci and gryi. Each student has the opportunity to hold a brain in the palm of a hand, and to guess how much it weighs. The average human brain weighs about 2 pounds.*

*Students are exposed to lectures and hands-on activities that deal with the brain, memory, and learning implications. For example, one recent class found students rotating through a series of stations that included comparing animal brains in jars, viewing a functional MRI scan of brain activity during a visual task, finding one's own blind spot, and concluding with examining and labeling several human brains. Lectures and activities progressed towards students developing an understanding of the brain and how learning occurs. The course concluded with each student producing an instructional design for the classroom using the learning theories to support their work.*

*Recent neuroscience research has unveiled a surprisingly plastic adult brain. Long-held dogma that new brain cells are never born in adults has been challenged by work from the laboratories of Fred Gage and Peter Eriksson, scientists who found neurogenesis in the human brain; although what these new brain cells do is still a mystery. Imaging studies have shown that with training and physical therapy, cortical areas can be recruited to take over the job of nearby brain regions that have sustained damage. Now it is known that the prefrontal cortex, arguably the part of the brain that makes us most "human," is still developing in the late teens and early twenties. Studies in animals, and now in people, have shown that environmental factors and prior experience can greatly influence the patterns of activity in the brain and even influence gene expression. As educators we want to take advantage of this flexibility, but how can we tap into these potential learning opportunities?*

*Knowledge is key. Beginning with increasing the level of awareness and knowledge of brain function for our teachers, eventually we can bring the results of recent brain research into the classroom. Already studies of autistic spectrum disorders, dyslexia, and attention-deficit disorders are improving the teaching practices for children with these disorders. But we also stand to benefit the average and gifted child in the classroom, by applying findings about the environment and learning, about the role of attention and how to maintain it, and about maximizing memory. Our goal is to use recent research to tune teaching techniques and optimize learning.*

*Dr. Teena Moody and Dr. Shawn K. Smith*
*Chapman University Magazine, Fall 2004*

## Theories On How We Learn

As a teacher or team of teachers, you are probably reading this book to become better at your craft. Undoubtedly, one of the ways to do so is to understand how humans learn. The following chart summarizes some of the many schools of thought and research on human learning. The highlighted names and theories are those we discuss in this book; the others are included to indicate their significant contributions to theories of learning.

| Behaviorist Theories | Cognitive Memory Theories | Cognitive Development and Interaction Theories |
|---|---|---|
| Classical Conditioning | Gestalt Theory | *Piaget's Cognitive Development Theory* |
| Watson's Behaviorism | Lewin's Theory | |
| Hull's System | Tolman's Theory | *Vygotsky's Cultural-Historical Theory* |
| Guthrie's Theory | *Information-Processing Theory* | |
| Thorndike's Connectionism | *Gange's Learning Conditions* | *Bandura's Social-Cognitive Theory* |
| *B.F. Skinner's Operant Conditioning* | | Motivation Theories |

### Behaviorist Theories

Early views of behaviorist theories assert that consequences influence learner behavior. Behavioral psychology dominated the educational landscape for the first part of the century. B.F. Skinner, the most well known of the behaviorists, argued that learning is a direct result of change in behavior and emphasized the critical role that positive reinforcement plays.

## Piaget's Cognitive Development Theory

The Swiss psychologist, Jean Piaget, helped influence our understanding of intelligence and cognitive development when he challenged long-held views about IQ. Trained under Theodore Simon, who helped devise some of the first tests to measure intelligence, Piaget became particularly interested in the errors children were making on these tests. He later came to believe that the particular errors the children were making were less important than the reasoning deployed by the children as they considered their choices.

Imagine, for example, having two rolled up balls of clay in your hand, each of equal size and proportion. You hold out both balls and allow a child sitting next to you to see and touch both. You ask the child, "Which one has more clay?" The child correctly responds, "They are the same." Now imagine, in the presence of the child, taking one of the balls and flattening out the entire ball like a pancake. Placing both objects in front of the child, one newly-flattened ball and the original ball still rolled, you again ask the child, "Which one has more clay?" This time the child responds, "That one" pointing at the newly-flattened, but larger surface area ball. While the balls of clay changed in shape, they did not change in volume. What Piaget found interesting is the child's reasoning behind the response.

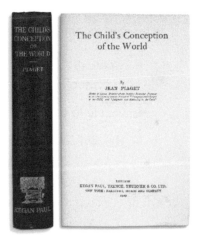

*Figure 5.4 is a first-edition, first-printing of Piaget's The Child's Conception of the World.*

In Piaget's **Theory of Cognitive Development,** he studied the correlation between a child's cognitive development and age. With this research, Piaget found four sequential stages of a youth's cognitive development and that a child will progress through each at an individualized pace. The four stages are as follows: Sensorimotor (0–2 years); Preoperational (2–7 years); Concrete operational (7–11 years); and Formal Operational (11–15 years).

The following characteristics are unique to the **Sensorimotor** stage of Piaget's cognitive development. The child:

▶ Begins to make use of imitation, memory and thought

▶ Begins to recognize that objects do not cease to exist when they are hidden

▶ Moves from reflex actions to goal-directed activity

The following characteristics are unique to the **Preoperational** stage of Piaget's cognitive development, in which the child:

▶ Gradually develops use of language and the ability to think in symbolic form

▶ Is able to think operations through logically in one direction

▶ Has difficulties seeing another person's point of view

The following characteristics are unique to the **Concrete Operational** stage of Piaget's cognitive development, during which the child:

▶ Can solve concrete (hands-on) problems in logical fashion

▶ Grasps laws of conservation and can classify and seriate

▶ Understands reversibility

The following characteristics are unique to the **Formal Operational** stage of Piaget's cognitive development. The child now:

▶ Can solve abstract problems in logical fashion

▶ Becomes more scientific in thinking

▶ Develops concerns about social issues and identity

Critical learning over the last 20 years however, has begun to challenge aspects of Piaget's theory on cognitive development. Many tasks once documented as solved by children only in Piaget's operational stage have been solved by children in the pre-operational stage. However, in those studies, various adjustments were made or introduced in the experiment. This leaves many wondering about the role environment plays as children progress through Piaget's stages of cognitive development—and gives educators hope about the positive role a teacher's classroom environment can have as children develop.

## Vygotsky's Cultural-Historical Theory

Another critic of intelligence tests, Soviet psychologist Lev Vygotsky, helped advance our understanding of cognitive development when he observed and documented a child's *zone of proximal development.*

Vygotsky's **zone of proximal development (ZPD)** theory is the distance between what a learner has already mastered (actual level of development) and what can be achieved when provided with educational support (potential development). This "zone" is where the student is actually learning. According to Vygotsky, tasks and activities should

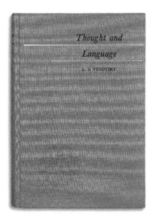

*Figure 5.5 is a first edition and printing of Vygotsky's Thought and Language.*

*5.6 is a first edition of Piaget's comments on Vygotsky's work.*

be just beyond the learner's reach, and the learner should be provided the right support system to complete the desired task. This support system can take on many different forms: *the teacher, classmates, parents, or other knowledgeable people.*

## Scaffolding

**Scaffolding** occurs when the learner is provided a bridge between what they currently know and the desired outcome on the task or activity. There are many different ways teachers can scaffold instruction to meet the learner in their zone of proximal development. Understanding and customizing instruction based upon each student's "zone" is also referred to as a student's readiness level.

| | Piaget | Vygotsky |
|---|---|---|
| **Theoretical Assumptions (How Learning is Fostered)** | Children progress through an invariant sequence of four stages that reflect qualitative differences in children's cognitive abilities. | Instruction should be scaffolded in the *zone of proximal development*. Student readiness levels deeply affect learning. |
| **Theoretical Principles** **Cognitive Representation** | Stages of Cognitive Development: Sensorimotor; Preoperational; Concrete Operational; Formal Operational | Developmental Method<br>- Mediation through signs<br>- Emphasized culture<br>- Based in human activity |
| **Learning and Developmental Readiness** | Children construct their own knowledge in response to their experiences, learning on their own without adult intervention. Children are intrinsically motivated to learn and do not need rewards from adults to motivate learning. | Understand and know each learner's readiness level. Customize instruction within the zone of proximal development. |
| **Instructional Methods and Strategies** | - Rich learning environment that supports activity.<br>- Encourage interaction with peers.<br>- Make learner aware of conflicts and inconsistencies in their thinking. | - Engage learner in medium-level questions to provoke cognitive conflict.<br>- Involve learners in inquiry and problem solving.<br>- Provide a bridge between what the child knows and the desired learning outcome. The bridge should be just within reach of the learner. Assist learner in making connections with what they know, including past experiences. |

## Bandura's Social Cognitive Theory

Albert Bandura added to the theories of cognitive development when his research studied the effects that social interaction has on learning and memory.

> *Learning would be exceedingly laborious, not to mention hazardous, if people had to rely solely on the effects of their own actions to inform them what to do. Fortunately, most human behavior is learned observationally through modeling: from observing others one forms an idea of how new behaviors are performed, and on later occasions this coded information serves as a guide for action. Social Learning Theory, 1976*

Bandura's **Social Learning Theory** suggests that individuals learn from one another through observation, imitation, and modeling. Bandura believes that learning is defined as the acquisition of symbolic representations in the form of verbal or visual codes that serve as guidelines for future behavior. In other words, a learner makes an observation while analyzing what is working and not working during the observation and then applies this knowledge to a behavior based on what they have learned.

The three core concepts of social learning theory are that first, people can learn through observation. Next, internal mental states are an essential part of this process. Finally, this theory recognizes that just because something has been learned, it does not mean that it will result in a change in behavior.

## The Information Processing Model

While Piaget and others mentioned above theorized on cognition and cognitive development, cognitive science or information processing psychology has now become one of the latest theories on how we learn. While Piagetian psychology sought to document and describe various stages of development through childhood, **information processing theory** seeks to understand memory and cognition down to the split second. It examines exactly how the brain receives, processes, and stores information.

The **Information Processing Model** attempts to describe why we are able to recall our childhood address but forget some of the points of a lecture attended a day ago. This model is used to explain how we receive information from our environment, process that information, and determine which information eventually gets stored for later use. The model, however, seeks to explain that phenomena as it is happening, rather than as stages of time where the intervals can span years.

The idea that the brain processes information much like a computer system has recently become a widely accepted analogy. Recent research using improved technologies has indicated a much more complex version of this linear model, noting

### Information Processing Model

*First, an input is registered from our senses or we retrieve stored information from long-term memory. Then, the information is sent to the thalamus for processing (except smell) and to the lobes of the brain (frontal, temporal, occipital, etc.) for further processing. Simultaneously, the input is sent to the amygdala. If it is a dangerous input, the brain activates other areas of the brain for immediate help.*

*Later, the input is sent to the hippocampus for a more nuanced processing and is held here during working memory.*

*At some point between working memory and long-term memory the hippocampus helps organize, classify, and store the input. It will help connect other memories to the input for storage, in essence, shaping the individual human mind. This is the subtle difference between the brain and the mind. Anatomically, humans have the same brain structure. The mind is what differentiates us as beings.*

that the brain is probably processing parallel information many times over, simultaneously. This parallel processing occurs using multiple neuropathways.

In 1985, Robert Stahl developed a model of the information processing system specifically for teachers. His model synthesized research from the 1960s and 1970s on cognition. David Sausa, in his book *How the Brain Learns* (2001) adapted the model and enhanced our understanding of information processing, going behind the early analogy of a computer system to one that addresses decision making and self-efficacy.

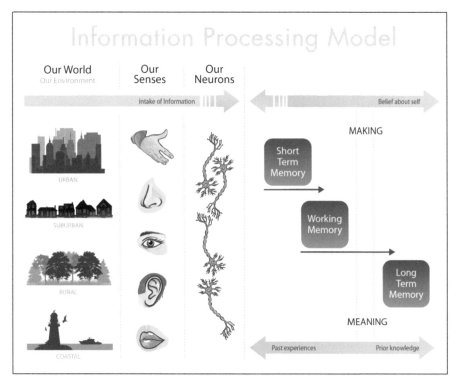

*Figure 5.7 is an adaptation of both models.*

As illustrated, the flow of information begins with inputs from our environment registered through our senses. The inputs, or electrical impulses, are a result of neurons firing along specific sensory pathways. The brain has a way of screening these inputs as they enter. It makes decisions as to which inputs are important and need attention and those that do not. For example, as I am writing this chapter, I am sitting in my home office with the door open. I can hear a family member in the kitchen putting dishes away. My brain has determined, as the sensory input of sound (dishes clanking) that this moment is not important for me to register in short-term memory, which means I will *not* work with it in working memory, nor eventually store it in long-term memory. When this book is published, the idea that dishes were being put away while I was writing Chapter 5 will probably be long forgotten (although now that I have chosen to write about it, given meaning to it, and formed an association will probably mean I will remember it!).

All incoming information, except smell, is sent to the thalamus first. The thalamus registers the sensory input for survival content and compares the input with the individual's past experiences to determine a level of importance before sending it along a neuropathway for processing. This all happens in less than a second. The brain processes millions of sensory inputs a day and most are not important; they will be dropped out of the processing system almost immediately. (Although noise from the kitchen continues, I eventually won't notice it. I'm sure you can recall times when background noise is annoying, but its ability to distract eventually fades.) This all occurs in short-term memory and usually only lasts for a couple of seconds.

As we mentioned earlier, the hippocampus is responsible for transmitting information from working memory to long-term memory and storage. It is constantly trying to make meaning from new information coming into the brain through our senses and checking the information with information that is already stored (prior knowledge and past experiences). Most inputs from our environment never make it to working memory. Think of all of the things you see or hear before you make it to your classroom each day: the car parked next to you in the street, the buildings you pass on the way, people at the bus stop. If you don't attend to the inputs they will be dropped from the processing system.

At the beginning of this chapter, I shared a memory from over a decade ago. As I recounted that memory, down to the clothes I was wearing, I had distinct memories of the smell of the train station, trains, and their tracks. Our sense of smell is the only sensory input from our environment that enters the brain, skips over the thalamus, and goes directly to the hippocampus for processing. This is often why memories from our past are associated with a sense of smell. For instance, walking into a bakery now that has just prepared fresh blueberry pies reminds you of your grandmother who loved blueberry pies. The smell triggers memories of your grandmother and days you spent with her as a child.

Our other four senses, however, first process environmental inputs through the thalamus where our brain will determine whether or not to send it to working memory. Some inputs never make it while others do. Working memory has been described by some as the consciousness of the information processing system. Whenever we are actively trying to remember or consciously thinking about something, we are doing so in working memory. If input makes it to working memory, there are three options: it can be lost or forgotten; the input can be retained in working memory for a short period of time by repeating it over and over (rehearsing); or the input can be transferred into long-term memory for storage (Eggen and Kauchak).

Working memory is limited in capacity and duration. Past studies have indicated that working memory can hold between five and nine pieces of information.

There are several strategies that aid in holding information in working memory. **Chunking** refers to grouping information. For example, it is easier to remember the phone number 910-6645 than it is to remember the digits 9106645. There are many educational strategies that aid in a student's ability to transfer information from working memory into long-term memory. We discuss these later in Instructional Strategies.

| Brain Learning Summary and Learning Theory Assumptions | | | |
|---|---|---|---|
| | **Behaviorist** | **Cognitive Memory** | **Cognitive Development and Interaction** |
| **General Assumptions and Key Concepts** | **Classical Conditioning:** a theory of learning in which a neutral stimulus becomes conditioned to elicit a response through repeated pairing with an unconditioned stimulus. **Operant Conditioning:** a theory of learning in which presenting reinforcement contingent upon a response emitted in the presence of a stimulus to increase the rate or likelihood of occurrence of the response. | How the brain takes in information is important. How the brain processes information affects how the information will be stored. Children learn in different ways. Depth of understanding content spans many levels. | Children develop skills in predictable sequences. Children are not passive learners. They construct meaning from experiences. Children are social. These interactions stimulate cognitive development. Beliefs about one's self influence learning. |
| **Key Terms** | Positive reinforcer Negative reinforcer Behavioral objectives Contingency contracts | Attention Encoding Elaboration Retrieval Schemata | Self-efficacy Modeling Observational Learning Teacher Modeling Zone of Proximal Development Motivation |
| **Theorists** | B.F. Skinner | Robert Stahl, Robert Gange | Jean Piaget, Lev Vygotsky, Albert Bandura |

## Pedagogy Research

### Defining and Understanding Pedagogy

The literature about pedagogy is rich with definitions and examples of the word or concept. Most refer to pedagogy as the process of teaching and includes just about everything that goes into planning a lesson. Pedagogy is often the umbrella term that incorporates the order in which a lesson is planned, instructional strategies, management techniques, teaching behaviors, curriculum design, learning experiences children have with the curriculum, and so on. While all of these larger teaching components are important (and should be taken into consideration when planning) we use pedagogy in a more granular way: **pedagogy** is the specific steps or elements of the lesson and the specific order of those elements used to build/scaffold or create learning for students.

Pedagogy has a direct link to learning theory. For the last several hundred years, philosophers and researchers have written about and studied various approaches to learning. Teachers use these learning theories as a foundation for designing effective lessons.

The first step in designing an effective lesson is understanding the choices available. Have a student-centered rationale for the pedagogical choices you make. Examine the content you are teaching and the key learnings students are expected to know and do. Then make an informed decision about the most effective pedagogical choice for that lesson. A healthy learning environment for students often has a myriad of pedagogical offerings each day or over the course of a week or unit.

Following the selection of pedagogy, the teacher designs several other larger components in teaching which will be described in the coming sections and chapters of this book.

# Three Popular Approaches:
# Direct Instruction, Constructivist and Inquiry-Based

## Direct Instruction

Although direct instruction has its roots in several learning theories, **behaviorism** is the most notable. B.F. Skinner argued that learning is a direct result of change in behavior (1953) and positive reinforcement plays a critical role in this. Skinner's aspects of behaviorism (1968) mirror many of the principles of direct instruction.

Robert Gange helped advance our understanding of learning when he wrote about and described the conditions for learning (Gange, 1985; Gange and Driscoll, 1988). His nine phases of learning can be linked to both direct instruction and information processing theory.

Studies over the last half century have examined if direct instruction has had an impact on effective teaching. These studies have looked specifically at direct instruction's influence on special education students, academically at-risk students, and high-performing students. Furthermore, some studies have examined direct instruction's link to behavioral characteristics like independence, curiosity, and creativity. Other studies have considered the link between direct instruction and affective skills like self-esteem, self-efficacy, beliefs, and social skills (Anderson, Evertson, and Brophy, 1979; Darch and Carnine, 1986; Medley, 1979; Paik, 2002)

Probably one of the most well-known authorities on direct instruction is Madeline Hunter. Her work spanned the 1960s, 70s, 80s, and 90s. She has written extensively on motivation, reinforcement, retention, and transfer— documenting each with precision in lesson design. Hunter's landmark work *Mastery Teaching* (1982) had significant influence on direct instruction's place in learning theory and pedagogy. It helped shaped teaching practices, observations, and evaluations throughout the 1980s.

Overall, direct instruction's impact on effective teaching has been mixed. While some studies like Grapko (1972) found that low-performing students did better with this pedagogical approach, other findings asserted that high-performing students benefitted more from open-ended, non-directed pedagogical approaches (Solomon and Kendall, 1979). Direct instruction was also found to be effective in teaching high school chemistry to students with learning disabilities (Woodward and Noell, 1991). Either way, it appears context matters immensely. While research indicates direct instruction's benefit with certain groups of students or for certain types of tasks, it also points towards the success of other theories over direct instruction.

## When to Use Direct Instruction

Direct instruction has been shown to be particularly effective when teaching specific procedures, basic skills tasks, or where the level of mastery needs to be critiqued for step-by-step accuracy. For example, if you want to teach someone how to make a specific dish while cooking, first modeling the task and followed by structured practice and feedback would be a viable way for the learner to learn to cook the meal. However, if you wanted the learner to create their own new recipe, direct instruction might not be the best pedagogical choice to make at that moment— a more experimental design might better serve the learner.

Direct instruction has also been shown to be most effective when the learning task is at the lower end of the Cognitive Growth Targets. It is documented that learning tasks that involve retrieval of information or comprehension of new material is best learned using direct instruction.

| Learning Theory | Direct Instruction Pedagogical Approach |
|---|---|
| ▶ Gain Student Attention | ▶ Opening |
| ▶ Present Stimulus | ▶ State Objective |
| ▶ Recall Prior Knowledge | ▶ Activate Prior Knowledge |
| ▶ Provide Learning Guidance | ▶ Teacher Modeling |
| ▶ Elicit Performance | ▶ Guided Practice |
| ▶ Provide Feedback | ▶ Independent Practice |
| ▶ Assess Performance | ▶ Check for Understanding |
| ▶ Cue Retrieval | ▶ Closing: Summarize Key Learning |

## Constructivist Theory

The **Constructivist Theory,** at its core, asserts that humans learn best by constructing their own meaning from experiences. Meaning can be constructed individually as the learner challenges assumptions from past experiences with learning from new experiences. Meanwhile, when two or more people share experiences and try to construct meaning together, by challenging each other's assumptions through their new experiences, group learning becomes the center of knowledge.

## Individual and Social Constructivism

Within **Individual Constructivism,** the learner creates knowledge and constructs concepts individually. Learning becomes an internal process as the learner struggles to solve a problem. Similar is **Social Constructivism,** in which knowledge is constructed and distributed as members of a group. Co-participants develop and construct meaning by challenging each other's view points through shared experiences.

*We see the Constructivist Theory's core principles play out in classrooms when teachers are intentional. Constructivist lessons often use primary sources, raw data, manipulatives, and real-world applications.*

*The lessons pose open-ended questions and allow for rich discussion between students. Student-to-student academic talk becomes the centerpiece of the lesson. The teacher's ability to **listen intently** to student responses is an important element in lesson success.*

Constructivist lessons are designed to allow students to share their understanding of the concept first, before the teacher shares their own understanding through modeling. As students explain their thinking of the concept, both with the teacher and each other, the lesson design seeks elaboration of student responses, probing students to go deeper in their thinking by challenging their assumptions. Note that this method requires teachers to become skilled at sufficient wait time while students process and construct their responses. Critics of constructivism argue that students do not have the ability to construct their own meaning from their misconceptions, hindering their learning.

It could be argued that one of the most influential books in education over the last half century was Brooks and Brooks' *In Search of Understanding: The Case for Constructivist Classrooms* (1993). In their thoughtful work, Brooks and Brooks describe and detail what a constructivist classroom looks and feels like. Their description of students assembling their own understanding of information and constructing their own conceptual understanding of material through well-crafted and planned experiences provided us with valuable insights on the application of constructivism in our classrooms. We recommend reading this important work.

## When to Use a Constructivist Lesson

Constructivist lessons provide students with experiences that often times challenge their assumptions of the world. In contrast to direct instruction, constructivist lessons push students' thinking into the future by designing a set of experiences for them to construct their own meaning from things, sometimes resulting in the production of new knowledge or information.

While direct instruction focuses student attention on mastery of knowledge already discovered, students most benefit from a constructivist lesson when the learning objectives extend to the higher levels of the Cognitive Growth Targets. Tasks that involve analysis, reasoning or creating might be most effective if experienced through a constructivist lesson design.

| Learning Theory: Constructivist | Pedagogical Approach |
| --- | --- |
| ▶ Learning is socially constructed | ▶ Engagement |
| ▶ Negotiating the rules of discourse | ▶ Exploration |
| ▶ Participating in the exchange of views | ▶ Explanation |
| ▶ Questioning and explaining | ▶ Extensions |
| ▶ Apprenticeship | ▶ Elaboration |
| ▶ Analyses from the individual perspective | ▶ Evaluation |

## Inquiry-Based Learning Theory

What does the research tell us about **inquiry-based pedagogy?** A number of studies have documented inquiry-based learning and its positive effect on student attitudes towards science, higher-order thinking skills, creativity, and learning the scientific method for both the sciences and social sciences. In all of these studies there was an overall positive effect on either achievement or attitude (Schrenker, 1976; Bredderman, 1983; Karplus and Their, 1967).

Critics of inquiry-based pedagogy often describe the enormous amount of classroom time it takes, and many teachers feel they do not have enough time to plan inquiry-based lessons. Some critics have even suggested that the instruction can be too demanding for students and has little impact on their everyday lives (Krajcik, et al., 2001).

According to Heather Banchi and Randy Bell in *"The Many Levels of Inquiry"* (2008), there are four levels for inquiry-based pedagogy in science education. These four levels vary in complexity and cognitive demand for learners. The lowest level of cognitive demand is **confirmation inquiry,** in which students are provided the inquiry-based question and method and the results are known in advance. This form of inquiry is often used to reinforce a concept that has already been introduced or to introduce students to investigations and inquiry.

The second is **structured inquiry,** in which the question and methods are given to the students in advance, but students generate the explanations by testing and observing their own hypothesizes. The third is **guided inquiry,** in which the teacher provides students with only the question. Students then develop methods to answer the question and carry out the procedures by testing and recording their hypotheses.

Finally, the fourth and highest form of inquiry and cognitive demand is **open inquiry**. Considered by many to be inquiry in its purest form, students derive everything on their own, beginning with the question of inquiry.

## When to Use an Inquiry-Based Lesson

Depending on the content you are teaching, some lessons are better with an inquiry-based approach. Make sure you have the time because you will also need to devote more time to planning and teaching inquiry-based lessons than a direct instruction approach requires.

If your intention is to design a lesson that requires students to analyze, reason, or create, then an inquiry-based approach may be the best pedagogical choice.

| Inquiry-Based Learning Theory | Inquiry-Based Pedagogical Approach |
|---|---|
| ▶ Determine a Focus Question | ▶ Question |
| ▶ Create a Hypothesis | ▶ Wonder |
| ▶ Foster an Experimental Design | ▶ Consider and Predict |
| ▶ Collect, Analyze and Record Data | ▶ Develop |
| ▶ Data Analysis | ▶ Observe and Record |
| ▶ Find Conclusions and Generalize Results | ▶ Discover and Communicate |
| ▶ Share Findings | |

## Which Comes First?

For many, many years we believed that before students could analyze information, reason with it, or create something new they *first* had to master the lower levels of memorization and comprehension of the content. In other words, they had to grasp the content core *before* they could use it. In fact, it is actually the opposite. This sequencing of instructional objectives—retrieval before comprehension, comprehension before analysis, analysis before reasoning—has been disproven in recent learning theory research (Resnick, 2007). Using knowledge as it is being learned increases students' ability to secure the learning objectives.

Today's instruction should require our students to analyze the vast amount of information available, reason with it, and look for new and innovative ways to solve complex, real-world problems *while* they are retrieving and trying to comprehend a subject's core knowledge.

## Instructional Strategies Research

In 1998, Robert Marzano detailed the work of researchers at the Midcontinent Research for Education and Learning (McREL) in their effort to analyze the effect of instructional strategies on student learning. Their meta-analysis of a number of different studies grouped certain instructional strategies used by teachers. The specific strategies used on the experimental group were then examined for an *effect* of achievement relative to a standard deviation increase or decrease. This was then compared to the control group. This meta-analysis concluded by identifying instructional strategies that have a high probability of increasing the achievement levels of students who have been exposed to a teacher using these specific strategies during instruction. Marzano, Pickering, and Pollack, in their book *Classroom Instruction that Works* (Marzano, Pickering, and Pollack, 2001), translated the meta-analysis into concrete examples for teachers.

In the study they described nine categories of strategies, which became the basis for *Classroom Instruction that Works.*

1. Identifying similarities and differences
2. Summarizing and note taking
3. Reinforcing effort and providing recognition
4. Homework and practice
5. Nonlinguistic representations
6. Cooperative learning
7. Setting objectives and providing feedback
8. Generating and testing hypotheses
9. Questions, cues, and advanced organizers

While the book is a helpful tool for teachers as they plan strategies, we have often found that teachers who plan the instructional strategy as the main point of their lesson do not maximize the potential of every lesson and miss opportunities to deliver high-quality instruction. Marzano himself acknowledges that the book does not address other aspects of pedagogy.

## Guiding Questions

▶ Have you thought about the connections between learning theory and lesson planning?

▶ How do you select the best pedagogical approach to use when teaching a lesson?

▶ Can you generalize how certain students will respond to instruction based on how familiar they are with the content?

▶ How do you choose instructional strategies to support student learning?

▶ How do you think about students' learning preferences when planning your lessons?

## Connecting to Classroom Practice

Research on the brain and learning theory and new studies shed new insights on how humans learn, giving teachers the information we need to build learning theory into our classroom practices.

Be intentional in your design. **Our message is simple: have a student-centered rationale for the instructional choice you make for each lesson you teach.** Examine the content you are teaching and the key learnings that students are expected to know and be able to do. Then make an informed decision about the most effective

**Choosing an Effective Pedagogy**

*When choosing the most effective pedagogical approach for each lesson, consider the following:*

*The **content** you are teaching. Some content is better with certain pedagogical approaches.*

*The **thinking** you want students to do. Some pedagogical approaches lend themselves to higher-order thinking.*

*How **engaged** you want students to be. Some pedagogical approaches require student-to-student engagement, while others are more teacher-directed.*

*How much **time** you have for the lesson. Some approaches need more time.*

pedagogical choice for that lesson. A healthy learning environment for students often consists of a myriad of pedagogical offerings each day or over the course of a week.

| | Pedagogy | Instructional Strategies | High-Impact Teaching Behaviors |
|---|---|---|---|
| **Definition** | Pedagogy is the way in which you build learning within a lesson: the order of and the specific steps or elements of the lesson that will be used to build/scaffold/ create the learning experience for students. | Instructional choices that support the pedagogy, thinking, and learning goals selected for the lesson. Instructional strategies assist in setting up the learning experience students will go through during the lesson. | Specific teaching behaviors that have a positive correlation (causal relationship) with student achievement. |
| **Example** | Constructivist | Open-ended/probing questioning<br><br>Think-Pair-Share | Sufficient wait time<br><br>Effectively guiding incorrect answers |

## When to Use Specific Instructional Strategies

We have organized instructional strategies, based on learning theories and brain research, into three categories that are a direct link to how the brain functions and learns. As we have described, architecting instructional design is a complex process. Selecting purposeful instructional strategies is one element in the pedagogy of instruction.

1. **Priming the Brain and Activating Prior Knowledge:**
   The Night Before, The Hook, Probing Questions/Mild Controversy, The Curiosity Strategy, State Random Facts

2. **Working Memory and Rehearsal:**
   Metaphors and Analogies, Spacing Effect, Chunking, Rehearsal and Music, Mnemonic Devices, Role Play Strategy

3. **Making Learning Meaningful:**
   Share Strategy, Share and Respond Strategy, Primary Source Strategy, Student-Selected Graphic Organizers, Reflection, Cornell Notes, Trace My Thinking Strategy

# Brain-Based Instructional Strategies

| **Brain-Based and Instructional Strategies** |
|---|
| **The Night Before**—Allows students to preview new content before it's introduced in class. Can be used in many ways and with some or all students. Powerful with students lacking significant background knowledge, which can hinder motivation during a lesson. Cue students in a way that explicitly links this new content with content that has already been taught or something in the student's background that relates. Present new content in graphic organizer form, visuals, and imagery, and cue the students with questions or statements that link the visual to past experience. |
| **The Hook**—A brief moment at the beginning of the lesson that draws your students into the content. The Hook creates excitement and independent student discussion about the lesson. It captures student attention and primes the brain for learning. The Hook should not be used as an entire lesson itself; most are only the first 3–5 minutes of a lesson—could be as short as 10 seconds. Every lesson does not need a hook. (See Lights, Camera—Action! below for an example). |
| **Probing Questions and Mild or Staged Controversy**—Stimulates curiosity about a concept while describing complex scenarios for students to think about. Staging a mild controversy includes opportunity for divergent thinking and can stimulate interest in a lesson and engage students. Use questions that force students to think about their opinions and use this energy to focus attention on the lesson objective. This strategy primes the brain for learning by motivating students to know more. Note that too strong a controversy can have an adverse effect on student engagement. |
| **The Curiosity Strategy**—Students are asked to wonder about the new content and generate good questions. Intentionally elicit questions by first asking students to be actively curious about the topic. |
| **The Random Facts Strategy**—Designed to gain student attention at the beginning of the lesson by stating interesting facts about the new content—stimulating the brain and making students inclined to want to learn. The random facts themselves have little value in isolation, but can be powerful attention-getters at the beginning of a lesson. For example, "A platypus is the only mammal to lay eggs," does not constitute knowledge, but provokes the desire for it. Facts are portable tidbits of knowledge for children. |
| **Sensory Pathways Strategy**—This strategy is connected to the Information Processing Theory and the architecture of the human brain. Incoming information (inputs) are processed in different parts of the brain (lobes) depending on the type of input. Our senses register the input and send it to the right part of the brain for processing. To create a rich learning environment that activates many regions in the brain for students, try to design experiences that use a variety of sensory inputs: sight, sound, touch, taste, smell. Some examples: drawing pictorial representations of content, kinesthetic mimicking of procedural, conceptual, or declarative knowledge, music, accessing a range digital content. |

| Making Learning Meaningful |
|---|
| **The Share Strategy:** The Share Strategy organizes students with partners or in groups multiple times throughout a lesson so students can actively process information with one another. |
| **Share and Respond Strategy (But Not You!):** Organize students with partners or groups many times throughout a lesson so students can process information with one another. Strategically facilitate whole group-structured, student-to-student academic talk—without interjecting your point of view. |
| **Primary Source Strategy:** Expose students to primary sources of content. Textbooks take a back seat to original documents. While this helps gain student attention, the core of this strategy is in asking students to interpret and make their meaning from the documents. |
| **Student-Selected Graphic Organizers:** Students self-select a graphic organizer to organize new content they are learning. This helps students make their own meaning from the information. |
| **Reflection:** Reflection is one of the most powerful instructional strategies and can be used in almost every lesson. Students should be asked to reflect on their learning often. |
| **Graphic Organizers:** One of the most common strategies, graphic organizers are a visual representation of content, concepts, and ideas that help the brain process and store information for later retrieval. |
| **Cornell Notes:** A note-taking system designed to help students organize, condense, and remember key concepts and information. In the 1950s, a professor at Cornell University developed a note-taking system to help his students organize and condense notes. The page is divided in two columns. In one, students take notes about key points of the lecture. In the other, students record unanswered questions and document key words they want to remember. Five to 10 lines are left at the bottom of the page. When the lecture is complete, students summarize main lecture ideas in the bottom space. Several adaptations of Cornell Notes exist. One is to have students draw an icon with key words and answered questions to help them in recall. |
| **Trace My Thinking or Thinking Footprints Strategy:** Just as footprints show where a person has been, the Thinking Footprints Strategy documents traces of thinking as students interact with new content. Students are taught to interact with a text by annotating their thinking along the pages. Highlighting, underlining, circling, and other marks are encouraged and modeled for students. Students leave footprints of their wonderings, questions, ideas, connections, and other things that come to mind as they read the text. |
| **The Role Play Strategy:** Students are asked to act out procedural content and explain in their own words how the procedure works. This kinesthetic instructional strategy combines movement, procedural knowledge, and students' own meaning of the content. Students can also be asked to role play how something functions and then to explain the procedure in their own words. Avoid surface level and make sure you ask students to go deep enough in their explanation. |

## Working Memory and Rehearsal

**Metaphors and Analogies:** A powerful way to develop a deeper understanding of new knowledge. Metaphors are used to describe similarities between the new content and unrelated content on the surface or literal level. Having students create analogies is the process of identifying relationships that exist between new and unrelated content.

**The Spacing Effect:** Best used over the course of an instructional cycle or unit. Present content many times, in small chunks, over the span of the cycle. Typically, the further the space of time with repeated opportunities for rehearsal and practice, the better the recall.

**Chunking:** Chunking organizes new content into small chunks. New content is broken down into small parts and introduced to students in small steps.

**Mnemonic Devices:** Used as an instructional strategy to aid the learner in recalling important information, these devices create associations between easy-to-remember constructs and new information.

**Rehearsal and Music:** Students create an original song using key concepts they want to remember. The song may be familiar or unfamiliar. Students practice singing the song in and outside of class. Alternately, students sing a familiar tune, with the original words replaced with lyrics that represent the key concepts and information students are learning. (See Lights, Camera—Action! below for an example of this strategy).

## Lights, Camera—Action!

We have seen several great examples of inspiring teachers use **The Hook** by telling a story, asking a question, making a provocative statement, or using a prop or costume.

When I was in 7th grade, my math teacher would occasionally begin the lesson by introducing the class to his friend, Mr. Kronkinhouse. He would then run into his classroom closet, quickly put on 1950s metal-frame glasses, a plastic nose, and a tweed overcoat. He would run back to the front of the classroom, and in his best British accent, introduce a new mathematical concept to us. After a quick intro he ran back to the classroom closet, changed out of the costume, and walked right back to the blackboard, never missing a beat. We loved it, and it totally hooked us in for the rest of the 50-minute class.

One teacher we observed had a clever way of helping students rehearse key content by **Setting It To Music.** Students were learning about the Pythagorean Theorem. Students created a song to help them remember the theorem.

*In a right triangle the sum of the hypotenuse*
*Is the sum of the square of the other two sides*
    *Same song second verse, it could get*
    *better but it's gonna get worse*

*In 30, 60 right triangle*
*This interesting fact you will see*
*The short leg is half the hypotenuse*
    *And the long is the short times the*
    *square root of 3*

*In a 45-45-90*
*It's isosceles you know that it's true*
*That means that both legs are equal*
    *Hypotenuse times the leg times the*
    *square root of 2*

## Blueprint Essentials

Cognitive neuroscience helps educators understand how the brain functions and learns.

Learning theories connect to brain development.

Pedagogy is the specific steps or elements of the lesson and the specific order of those elements used to build/scaffold or create learning for students.

Three popular pedagogical approaches are direct instruction, constructivist, and inquiry-based models.

21st century instruction requires teachers to offer a myriad of pedagogical choices when designing lessons. Some lessons are more effective using specific pedagogical approaches. It deeply depends on the types of thinking you want students to be doing.

Instructional strategies are strategically placed over the span of a lesson and are utilized to support the learner. Instructional strategies can be linked to how the brain functions and learns.

## Reflection and Action

### Reflection

▶ How does your understanding of how the brain processes information change the way you design instructional pedagogy?

▶ How does your understanding of the different learning theories make you think about the need to be intentional about instructional pedagogy? Why is it important for a teacher to be intentional about selecting instructional strategies?

▶ What are the different pedagogical options available to you? How do the different learning theories connect with instructional design?

▶ What is the difference between pedagogy and instructional strategies?

▶ How do instructional strategies relate to the different learning theories?

# In the Library

## The Brain and Learning

*A Mind at a Time: America's Top Learning
Expert Shows How Every Child Can Succeed* (2002)
Mel Levine

*How the Brain Learns* (3rd edition) (2005)
David A. Sousa

## Instructional Pedagogy

*In Search of Understanding:
The Case for Constructivist Classrooms* (1993)
Jacqueline Brooks and Martin Brooks

*Mastery Teaching:
Increasing Instructional Effectiveness
in Elementary and Secondary Schools, Colleges,
and Universities* (1982)
Madeline Hunter

*Engaging Readers and Writers with Inquiry
(Theory and Practice)* (2007)
Jeffrey Wilhelm

*Eight Essentials for Inquiry-Based Science, K–8,* (2005)
Elizabeth Hammerman

## Instructional Strategies

*Classroom Instruction that Works* (2001)
Robert Marzano

*Teach Like a Champion,* (2010)
Doug Lemov

# Journal Entry

**Experiencing and
Personalizing your Journey**

**Five Tiny Changes:** Over the course of the next month, challenge yourself to design one lesson from each of the pedagogical approaches described in this chapter. Select two new instructional strategies that you have never tried before and use them in your instruction.

**Journal:** After each lesson, describe how you felt teaching the lesson.

Describe how you and your students responded.

What does this have you wondering about in your classroom blueprint?

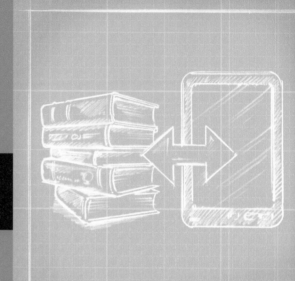

# Customizing
## 21st Century Learning

Know the 21st century learner,
leverage a range of advanced
technology tools that will provide
multiple learning pathways that
customize and enrich the learning
experience.

As we build upon Core Principle 1, the foundation of our blueprint, we introduce Core Principle 2, Customizing 21st Century Learning. We explore ways to transform our classrooms into highly customized learning spaces for students. We push the boundaries of where learning takes place by adding to our classroom blueprint virtual learning spaces. We explore how technological advances can be leveraged to help us accomplish this 21st century mission. We continue our discussion with two questions:

1. What does a 21st century classroom look like?

2. How will I plan for it?

Chapter 6—Customizing and Enriching Student Learning will demonstrate, using simple strategies, how customized teaching is effective in practice. We examine what customization can accomplish—and what it looks like—in real classrooms. We include topics that address blended learning and flipped instruction and help you make sense of these new practices.

Chapter 7—Instructional Materials and the 21st Century takes a look at the materials available to us as teachers. We examine the history of instructional materials and the publishing world and how these materials play a role in helping students meet learning expectations.

Chapter 8—Designing Classroom Instruction: The Blueprint brings together Chapters 1 through 7 and the planning process into a blueprint template for instructional design. Here is where you demonstrate your teaching architecture—and its impact on your physical classroom, your virtual opportunities, your colleagues, and your calendar.

## Core Principle 1
### Designing with Purpose

Design a blueprint for classroom instruction and strategically consider a range of choices to motivate student success.

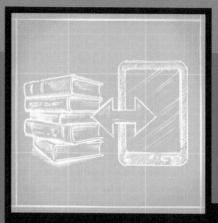

## Core Principle 2
### Customizing 21st Century Learning

Know the 21st century learner, leverage a range of advanced technology tools that will provide multiple learning pathways that customize and enrich the learning experience.

## Core Principle 3
### High-Impact Teaching Behaviors

Teach the blueprint by using a series of high-impact behaviors associated with student learning.

## Core Principle 4
### Managing Student Performance

From multiple sources, collect and analyze evidence of student learning to understand each student's mastery of specific content and readiness for new content.

## Customizing 21st Century Learning

Know your 21st Century Learner

Digital Learning Systems

### 21st Century Tools

### Learning Pathways

"Flipped Classroom"

Customize the Classroom Experience

Pedagogy & Lesson Design

Extend the Learning at Home

Leverage Social Media Academically

Facilitate Learning Anywhere, Anytime

© Modern Teacher Press 2012

# Chapter 6

# Customizing and Enriching

## Student Learning

# A Teacher's Story: Mr. Sullivan's Journey

*Mr. Sullivan is a sixth grade language arts and social studies teacher, and by all accounts he's a 21st century architect of learning for the students that are lucky enough to have him. That wasn't always the case. Let's take a look at Mr. Sullivan's journey. At 18, he left rural eastern Kentucky and headed off to New Hampshire on an academic scholarship to an Ivy League college. His four years were filled with student organizations, a semester abroad studying in Egypt, and he was captain of the tennis team.*

*At 22, Mr. Sullivan headed home and landed a job as a sixth grade teacher in a middle school near where he grew up. He always wanted to be a teacher and with a double major in history and English, he felt prepared for the content he was assigned to teach—language arts and social studies.*

*During his first year, Mr. Sullivan had little trouble establishing himself as the teacher: his classroom was well-managed, students rarely misbehaved, and most seemed to enjoy his classes. A typical social studies lesson would begin with students reading their textbook in class, note taking (he liked Cornell notes and used them in college), questions at the end of each chapter, or a worksheet that came with the textbook. He supported the in-class reading with a lecture. He worked hard on these lectures and used many resources from college. His lectures during the ancient Egypt unit were filled with pictures and occasionally artifacts from his time there. At the end of each unit, students were expected to do well on the chapter test (taken from text-provided materials as well as teacher-created). He spent the day before the test reviewing with students. Grades were determined by a combination of class participation, homework, and chapter tests.*

## Mr. Sullivan's Second Year

*During Mr. Sullivan's second year he began to diversify his approach to instruction. He supported the in-class reading with graphic organizers for students to fill in as they read and posted his notes online from the chapter so students could access them for extra help. He began to look for external resources to support other units like he did for the Egyptian unit (art, photographs, artifacts). He began to design lessons that did more than just ask students to memorize key vocabulary, dates, places, and people. He invited students to dress in clothes of the ancient civilization and allowed students to bring in food representative of that culture. He also began to incorporate video from National Geographic–and assigned a paper in language arts class (he had the same students for both subjects) comparing the video clips with the textbook. His school had recently purchased a digital learning system (DLS) and he found the video clips from National Geographic to be particularly interesting for his students. He was able to support his other units of study with still images of art and photography through the digital learning system as well. When it was time for the chapter tests he added student projects as part of the final grade. Students could choose from a list of five projects to culminate their unit: making a travel brochure, building a model of ancient architecture, creating a piece of art, making a board game of an ancient civilization, or writing a play.*

## Into 21st Century Learning—Mr. Sullivan's Third Year

*During Mr. Sullivan's third year, he began to customize student learning. He looked for ways to deepen their understanding of life in the ancient world at the onset of his unit planning. He began each unit by focusing in on a few key concepts students needed to know. He added principles and generalizations about each civilization that students would be expected to uncover through their study. Finally, he established a defined set of facts and vocabulary that students needed to remember and comprehend to be literate on the topic. This would also allow students to communicate about the content and push their thinking into analysis, reasoning, and creating during their study.*

*To hook them into the unit, he began by posing some essential questions to his class. The questions were often based on his own particular wonderings—and immediately created an intellectually-curious learning environment that students would explore together. He created a thirst for knowledge that was evident in his students' eagerness to get started. Altogether, his unit plan consisted of an architectural blueprint that listed the key vocabulary terms, facts, concepts, principles, and skills students would encounter in their study. His blueprint was held tightly together by his state standards, and in many cases went beyond it.*

*As his unit got underway, Mr. Sullivan continually used assessment data and student work to determine his students' **academic readiness** to learn, their **interests in the process** they are taking during their study, and their **intelligence preferences**. He had students monitor their own learning through a variety of methods and allowed them to make decisions about their own learning. There was built-in time for reflection and the units were always tied to real-world application in their own lives. Students were encouraged to think about their own place in this world by studying people from the past.*

## Refining The Build–Year Three and Beyond

*Mr. Sullivan's third year teaching about ancient Egypt had clearly evolved. The key concepts were about Egyptian culture, changes over time to the civilization, and how geography influenced life in the ancient world. Through the unit, students would explore and uncover generalizations and big ideas and form principles from their findings: culture is shaped by values and beliefs, resources, traditions, and customs. Life in the ancient world is interdependent. He established a list of key terms and facts: pyramids, Nile River, Queen Hatshepsut, pharaohs, mummy, King Tut, Rosetta Stone and more.*

*Units now began in class with Mr. Sullivan's essential questions and continued outside of the classroom using Web 2.0 tools. He intentionally selects both guided and open-inquiry pedagogy and links this approach to his essential questions. Because many of his students don't have access to the internet at home (although many have web-enabled cell phones), Mr. Sullivan arranged for students to have computer and internet access before and after school in his classroom and at the local public library. In rural Kentucky, long bus rides are common, so transportation issues limited students' abilities to stay after school. Nonetheless, Mr. Sullivan worked through the issues to make sure learning continued for his students outside of class. He set clear expectations about student collaboration, and monitored their virtual collaboration, and encouraged students to network with classmates and others from around the world.*

*Mr. Sullivan connected with a mentor teacher from the district to learn more about his school's digital learning system. He had already learned to incorporate videos, still images and audio into his lessons. He was able to search the system's vast amount of resources by his state standards, but he wanted to leverage more of its capabilities. He intuitively knew it could do more to customize for his students' learning but he wasn't exactly sure how. He met with the mentor teacher several times over that summer. Their focus was on the system's ability to help him differentiate and customize learning pathways for his students.*

*He created a new learning path for his students. For the first activity, students began their own research from either Mr. Sullivan's essential questions or they created their own. This interest-based learning activity allowed students to follow their own intellectual curiosity from a variety of directions. Mr. Sullivan began class by wondering how the effects of social media played a part in the revolution in Egypt the previous spring. He inquired about the relationship other Arab countries' uprisings had on Egypt. He asked if anyone thought there might be some connections and common themes to Egypt's relationships with their neighboring civilizations 5,000 years ago from those of today. Many students offered their own wonderings and the class ended with students documenting their essential questions and choosing to pursue one of the questions online.*

*For the second activity, students were asked to organize their collected information using a graphic organizer of their choice, and cite where the information came from. Students had to populate their collected information and sources into an Excel spreadsheet and analyze the credibility of their online sources. This was the beginning of their research that would be tracked and used throughout the unit.*

*The third task asked students to compare and contrast life in today's Egypt with life in ancient Egypt. Key terms, people, places, and documents (academic vocabulary) were introduced and students were responsible for generating effective paragraphs to convey their comprehension of the subject. Mr. Sullivan used both whole class and flexible networks to provide feedback to his students about their writing. Networks were both in-class and virtual. Student academic readiness levels were used to create his small networks. Students emailed their paragraphs to Mr. Sullivan and he gave both in-class and online feedback.*

*In reviewing his students' social studies writing he saw an opportunity to provide language arts lessons. He provided several mini lessons to various flex networks on grammar and spelling, appropriately scaffolding his instruction to meet his students' academic readiness levels. He tapped into the digital learning system his school had purchased and began to incorporate some of its other features. He created **digital playlists** that housed his mini lessons for grammar and spelling and assigned these playlists for small networks of his students to view **outside** of the classroom. He could assign these playlists based on each student's specific needs–some needed all of them, others a few of them, and others none of them. Technology was helping Mr. Sullivan differentiate in a new way. Each playlist included a quick, formative assessment so Mr. Sullivan could monitor the effect of his mini lessons with each student. Over the first semester he was able to create a dozen mini lessons for writing: grammar, spelling, conventions, voice, organization, and sentence fluency to name a few. During the second semester his grade level team became interested, created additional folders of mini lesson playlists, and their digital curriculum content had quadrupled by the end of the year.*

*As the unit continued, students used information from several of the previous activities to complete this task. All students were responsible for addressing a common set of questions: What influences do ancient Egyptian culture have on today's culture? What influences does American culture have on Arab culture? How are cultures interdependent? How has Egypt changed over the last 5,000 years? All students must meet criteria defined in a research rubric. Students publish their research from one of several Web 2.0 solutions: create a podcast, classroom wiki, or blog.*

*Finally, students used their published research and moved from a Web 2.0 solution to a task simulating the 3.0 Web. Students were asked to act as a data scientist and combine/mash-up Data Set A with Data Set B, both collected from their research throughout the unit, and determine what new valuable information they are now provided with that did not exist in either set individually. From these new insights, students created an email inbox based upon a major historical figure from the key terms in the unit. The inbox they would design would feature email communication from their historical figure to another historical figure from the ancient world.*

*Mr. Sullivan continued to assign customized playlists for his students to access outside of class in an effort to build their writing skills. He also created a new extension playlist for some of his more advanced writers. It included an audio interview of a famous author discussing writer's block and her strategies for overcoming it. He began by creating simple grammar lessons, but he could not stop thinking about the endless uses for customized playlists.*

*Mr. Sullivan connected with the school's art teacher and together they collaborated on an art extension of this final task. In art class, students designed and developed a screen shot of the email inbox that included advertisements targeted specifically for their historical figure based upon their new data set. Mr. Sullivan encouraged students to access the Excel spreadsheets and graphic organizers that stored their research, and data mine the information to create Web 3.0 (semantic web) advertisements aimed at their historical figure.*

*Mr. Sullivan continues to seek innovative ways to leverage technology to engage his students in higher-order thinking tasks and to customize their learning in and out of the classroom.*

## Your Take On Mr. Sullivan's Journey

What do you think about Mr. Sullivan? What does his journey have you considering about your own classroom practice? What elements of his plan did you connect with? Which technology resonated with you? Which technology needed clarifying? How do you think Mr. Sullivan improved his teaching effectiveness? This chapter is intended to help you connect 21st century learning (and its tools) into your instructional blueprint.

# Why We Do What We Do

Today's students are mobile, adaptive, and digital, which means we have even greater opportunity to facilitate learning anytime, anywhere. The new demands for our students require customized teaching for our learners—and for learning to be facilitated by networking our students with each other and others around the world. As we move into the second decade of the 21st century, the need for customized learning is more urgent than ever before.

## Towards a 21st Century Model of Teaching—Customized Learning

How do we move differentiated teaching into the 21st century? How do we design a blueprint like Mr. Sullivan's third year? This evolution begins by understanding *what* we want to differentiate for our learners, *how* we plan to do it, and what tools we have to make it happen.

Core Principle 2 **Customizing 21st Century Learning,** helps us customize and enrich learning experiences in our instructional plan. Customizing 21st century learning has its roots in differentiated teaching, but pushes the boundaries of traditional teaching and learning. It's preparing for anywhere/anytime learning by making customized plans based upon students' learning profile. It's networking students together with technology to accelerate and enrich their learning experience. It's creating multiple learning pathways for students using a myriad of technological options.

Customized learning, first and foremost, focuses on the learner by asking, "What does *this* learner need to be successful in the year 2030?" In the year 2030, the kindergarten class of 2012 will graduate from college. What skills will these kindergarten students need to succeed in the 21st century? Today's teachers will need to design a blueprint for learning that considers a range of choices for planning and teaching. **Customizing 21st Century Learning begins by knowing the 21st century learner, leverages a range of advanced technology tools that will provide multiple learning pathways that customize and enrich the learning experience.**

Consider these statistics from the Information Age:

▶ Data storage capacity doubles every 12 months.

▶ The 140 million archived documents in the U.S.
Library of Congress can now fit on a single digital device.

▶ Computer microchips double in processing speed
every 18 months.

▶ In 2008, Google announced it had indexed one trillion
web pages on their internet search engine.

▶ Every minute, 20 hours of video are uploaded onto YouTube.

▶ Every day, 50 million tweets are posted on Twitter.

▶ 247 billion emails are sent every day.

▶ Facebook has more than 400 million active users.

▶ 59% of Americans simultaneously use the internet
and watch television.

What do these facts, produced during the **Information Age,** mean for our
students now living in the **Conceptual Age**? What does it mean for our
teaching in this new millennium?

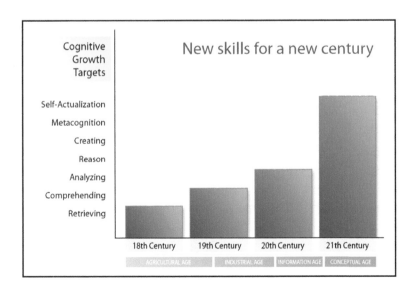

## Know the 21st Century Learner

In *Born Digital: Understanding the First Generation of Digital Natives,* John Palfrey and Urs Gasser discuss digital natives, or students born after 1980 and who have always known internet connectivity. The statistics above can be daunting for many of us born before 1980, but to our students, it is all they know.

*Know the 21st Century Learner by **understanding digital natives and 21st century skills.***

We begin by questioning what it means to know the 21st century learner: *What thinking skills will our student need to compete in the 21st century?* In Chapter 2, *Figure 2.3* showed the new skills students will need for this century. In past centuries, memorizing and retrieving facts was a vital part of school learning. Today, it's impossible and unnecessary. Students need a solid understanding of a subject's core facts, key principles, and theories, but *what* we ask students to do with this information matters. *How* we ask students to think using this information matters even more.

The Partnership for the 21st Century, a national organization that advocates for 21st century readiness for every student, defined the following necessary skills:

**Learning and Innovation Skills**

▶ Creativity and Innovation

▶ Critical Thinking and Problem Solving

▶ Communication and Collaboration

**Digital Literacy Skills**

▶ Information Literacy

▶ Media Literacy

▶ Information and Communication Literacy

**Career and Life Skills**

▶ Flexibility and Adaptability

▶ Initiative and Self-Direction

▶ Social and Cross-Cultural Skills

▶ Productivity and Accountability

▶ Leadership and Responsibility

These new learning and innovation skills are aligned to our Cognitive Growth Targets and can be directly linked to the selection of pedagogy in lesson design. For example, the Partnership for the 21st Century defines critical thinking and problem solving as the ability to reason effectively, use systems thinking, make judgments and decisions, and solve both familiar and unfamiliar problems. These skills require a level of *cognitive* demand that moves inward on the Cognitive Growth Targets. The tasks and activities we ask students to do should require heavy thinking.

*Know the 21st century learner by considering each student's learning profile:* **Academic readiness, interests, intelligence preferences, learning styles, gender, or culture.**

Customized learning is focused on the learner by asking, "What does *this* learner need to be successful in the 21st century?" Today's teacher then architects a blueprint for learning that considers what each student needs at *this* particular moment in instruction in order to reach the new 21st century skill set. The blueprint customizes the learning experience by considering students' learning profiles.

The concept of *differentiation* was made popular when Carol Ann Tomlinson published *The Differentiated Classroom: Responding to the Needs of All Learners* (1999). Like other words in our profession, practitioners mean different things by *differentiation*. We use Tomlinson's definition: "Differentiation is the systemic approach to planning curriculum and instruction for academically diverse learners." Typically, this means differentiating the content students learn, designing different processes for how they learn it, and multi-structuring the products they produce to demonstrate their mastery of the desired content. *Differentiating content* occurs as a result of students' academic readiness to learn the information or in response to students not yet mastering desired standards. Differentiating the process for how students learn the content can be managed by tapping into students' interests, learning styles or intelligence preferences.

**Learning profile** is a broad term used to combine four overlapping concepts related to a learner: learning style, intelligence preferences, culture, and gender (Tomlinson et al., 2003).

*Learning styles* are a preferred contextual approach to learning (Dunn and Dunn, 1992). Considerations for learning styles are adaptable in context, and include the following:

- Noisy or quiet classroom
- Lighter or darker classroom
- Warmer or cooler classroom
- Working on one task or several at one time
- Moving around or sitting still
- Working independently or in a group

Howard Gardner's *Theory of Multiple Intelligences* (discussed in Chapter 2) identifies other considerations for ***intelligence preferences*** within students' learning profiles. This hard-wired, neurological preference for thinking and learning can be categorized into eight categories below.

- Bodily-Kinesthetic Intelligence
- Interpersonal Intelligence
- Intrapersonal Intelligence
- Linguistic Intelligence
- Logical-Mathematical Intelligence
- Musical Intelligence
- Naturalistic
- Spatial Intelligence

We draw upon Tomlinson's definition of differentiation as well as her definition of a learner profile to **create a roadmap for customizing and personalizing instruction** for our 21st century learners. By strategically considering a student's learning style, intelligence preferences, culture, and gender, teachers can design instruction that blends together 21st century content and processes. Our students today are digital natives, need 21st century skills, have diverse academic readiness levels, and varying interests.

*Academic readiness* is determined by selecting an appropriate assessment or analyzing student work (discussed in Chapter 4) to zero in on students' Zone of Proximal Development (Vygotsky) from Chapter 5. In other words, *academic readiness is the distance between what a learner currently knows and the desired knowledge or skills you want the student to know or be able to do.* Unit and lesson plans are differentiated for students in a myriad of ways. Considerations for **academic readiness** include the following:

> ▶ Use a differentiated warm-up at the beginning of each lesson
>
> ▶ Use reading materials based upon students' reading levels
>
> ▶ Conduct mini lessons based upon students' strengths and weaknesses
>
> ▶ Use assessment data and student work to determine readiness
>
> ▶ Plan to re-teach several times throughout the unit in small groups
>
> ▶ Use data from previous units or district assessments to determine and monitor readiness
>
> ▶ Vary your instructional strategies to support students at different readiness levels
>
> ▶ Vary the complexity of resources students use to engage with content

Student interests are tied to motivation factors. Their motivation to engage in content is linked to their ability to attend to tasks. This often stems from their curiosity and affect toward the content. Students' emotions and feelings impact learning new content for a variety of reasons. Considerations for **student interests** include the following:

▶ Develop a survey, questionnaire, or check list to gauge student interests

▶ Connect interests to college and careers

▶ Share your own interests with students as a model

▶ Find small amounts of time to ask individuals about their own interests

▶ Use analogies, stories and metaphors that might connect to your students' interests

▶ Create flexible networks based upon heterogeneous and homogeneous student interests

▶ Provide different opportunities for students to share their interests

▶ Provide a range of digital and print resources related to student interests

▶ Provide models of expert work in areas of student interest

▶ Connect student goal-setting to interests

Customized learning leads to a move away from a one-size-fits-all approach to education (the industrial model) to a more personalized, connected approach, fostering:

▶ Increased interest and engagement levels

▶ Differentiated pacing

▶ Targeted instruction provided at student readiness levels (Zones of Proximal Development)

▶ Student ownership and motivation for their own learning— learning for learning's sake

▶ Multiple opportunities for students to master content in a variety of settings

Customized learning for students in your classroom begins by organizing for learning, leading to:

- ▶ Small, flexible groupings

- ▶ Students engaged in new content

- ▶ Students learning content at different times based upon readiness and mastery

- ▶ Flexible and adaptable physical settings

- ▶ Monitoring each child's learning plan and making adjustments based on engagement levels and content mastery

- ▶ The teacher facilitating learning by using a combination of pedagogical practices

- ▶ Strategic use of technology to deliver content

One final method of differentiating student learning is allowing student choice in what they produce. Differentiating what students produce as evidence of learning can bolster student motivation and engagement. Differentiating teaching based upon student academic readiness, interests, culture, and gender fosters an academic environment that is mobile, adaptive, and flexible and will meet the needs of our students.

Begin first by developing student learning profiles in your classroom. Learner profiles should include: learning styles, intelligence preferences, culture, gender, academic information, and interests. This profile can then be utilized to customize instruction in class and outside of class. Technology can be leveraged to personalize and customize instruction based upon the make-up of your classroom learner profiles.

## Advanced Technology Tools

"What does *this* learner need to be successful in 2030?" As your instructional design develops, consider a range of opportunities to push learning anywhere/anytime—creating a physical and virtual space for learning. Designing a brick and mortar classroom is just as important as preparing students for and organizing your virtual learning space. Use technology to help you customize learning for your diverse learners.

**Leverage advanced technology tools.**

It is time to strategically consider the second part of this concept: advanced technology tools. Customizing student learning is greatly eased with the impressive list of new technology available to us. The terms 1.0, 2.0, and 3.0 web solutions refer to the evolution of the web or internet experience and options. The rapid growth of the web and its uses has increased pathways for web-based interaction. This has greatly affected how the world communicates, accesses and uses information. The web evolution continues at laser-like speed with new innovations occurring daily. Today, new web 4.0 platforms are emerging. This evolution also affects how students learn and how we teach. The chart below captures the dynamic evolution of the web and its uses and attaches some commonly used language when referring to 1.0, 2.0, and 3.0 web solutions.

| 1.0 Web | 2.0 Web | 3.0 Web |
|---|---|---|
| Static | Dynamic | Semantic |
| Access/Find | Participate | Communal |
| Retrieve Information | Collaborate | Co-Creation |
| Email | Tagging | Adaptive to User |
| Research | Blogging | User Profiles |
| Web Forms | Social Networks | Portable/Personal |
| | Web Applications | Smart Applications |
| | | Content Management Systems |

## Educational Implications of 2.0 and 3.0 Web Solutions

| Technology and Web 1.0 | Web 2.0 | Web 3.0 |
|---|---|---|
| **Teacher Computer Workstation:** Defined as being off-limits to students; used to communicate and compile official classroom business.<br><br>**The Over-Head Projector:** A precursor to modern LCD projectors.<br><br>**The LCD Projector:** Quickly replacing over-head projectors to display at large scale, in color (and now 3-D), content that supports the classroom instructional materials.<br><br>**The Interactive White Board (IWB):** An opportunity for a teacher to cut all physical ties to the computer connected to the LCD projector and actively engage the whole group, small group, or individual students in instructional content including but not limited to manipulative and digital content.<br><br>**The Mobile Computing Lab:** Filled with either an entire classroom or small group set of laptops, netbooks, iPads, or iPods.<br><br>**The Document Camera:** The Elmo! The solution to an expensive color over-head projector. Inexpensive computer cameras can serve this task as well with many additional functions. | **Video or Audio Podcast:** Video or audio podcasting is a digital way to share ideas over video. They are pre-recorded and do not require an internet connection. Challenge students to create videos on varying research topics to share their knowledge. Other functions: digital portfolios, digital essays, video journal, video blog.<br><br>**Classroom Wiki:** Wikis are sites that allow creation and editing of interconnected websites. Wikis are a simple way to create teacher-to-student and student-to-student dialogue—and even group project development space, or classroom journaling—in an easy collaborative space.<br><br>**Blogging:** The word blog comes from a combination of the words web and log. Blogging is a way for students to communicate and give their work historical significance over a lifetime. Challenge students to create a portfolio of work and discussions around their accomplishments over a period of time. Other functions: classroom and student webpages can now be developed on a blog platform like WordPress.<br><br>**Social Media:** Social media is the engine of our students' communication with each other. Challenge your students to create Twitter posts interpreting an historic event—or Facebook pages about historical individuals.<br><br>**Google:** Google offers many Web 2.0 tools and sites and can make website development easy. Challenge your students to create robust web pages around academic content.<br><br>**The Student Response System:** Clickers! These devices allow for real-time student response and assessment. | **iPad:** Is a line of tablet computers designed and marketed by Apple Inc., primarily as a platform for audio-visual media, including books, periodicals, movies, music, games, apps and web content.<br><br>**Smart Phone:** Is a mobile phone built on a mobile operating system, with more advanced computing capability and connectivity than a feature phone.<br><br>**Adaptive Assessments:** Are dynamic and adapt in real time as students select their answers. Typically, there is one scale, broken down into equal intervals and are independent of student grade level.<br><br>**Learner Profile:** Student information used to customize instruction based upon their academic readiness, interests, learning styles, intelligence preferences, culture and gender.<br><br>**Digital Learning System:** Is a multi-user, customized learning environment where educators can create, store, reuse, meta-tag, manage, and deliver digital learning content from a central object repository. It allows for the ability to customize instruction through the integration of unique learner profiles and intentional pedagogical choices.<br><br>**Application Design:** Mobile apps are some of the most advanced and useful tools available. There are thousands of education-related apps available that can help customize your instruction. |

## Multiple Learning Pathways

### "The Flipped Classroom"

By the end of the first decade in the 21st century, more than three million students had taken an online course. Ten years prior, only 45,000 students from kindergarten to grade 12 had taken a course online. In Clayton Christensen's provocative 2008 book, Disrupting Class, he predicts that by the end of the 2020, over 50% of high school courses will be delivered online. What does that mean for education? What does that mean for classroom teachers? For teachers who were not born digital and are preparing blended learning to teach students who were, these predictions are scary and exciting.

*Create multiple learning pathways.*

Let's go back in time for a second, to Valentine's Day in 2005. On February 14, 2005 the domain name www.youtube.com was activated. Over the course of the next few months YouTube began its initial development and on April 23, 2005 the first video *Me at the Zoo* was uploaded and shared. Fast forward two years, to the spring of 2007, and two high school chemistry teachers in Colorado began experimenting with screen-capturing software. They were able to record their live lessons and post them online for their students to view. For Jonathon Bergmann and Aaron Sams it helped solve some of their initial hurdles with student absenteeism. Over the next year they began to refine their videos and lectures and could see unlimited potential with this new idea.

While all of this was happening, Salman Khan began recording math lessons to help tutor his cousin. He too would post his teaching videos on the web for his cousin to see. Little did he know he know the world would join in. By 2012, his 3,000 video lessons would be viewed over 140 million times, averaging 100,000 views a day. Tutoring his cousin with video lessons became the genesis of Khan Academy.

Innovations in technology also helped create a perfect storm. Apple would launch a line of products that enabled mobile learning. It wasn't until April of 2010 that the first iPad was released.

Jonathon Bergmann and Aaron Sams, the two chemistry teachers in Colorado, were early adopters of "flipped" instruction. For them, it was about using technology as an instructional tool. They understood well that it was about leading with, and being intentional in, their pedagogical choices first and then leveraging technology to support their goals. Various media outlets began running with the "flipped" term although it would take Daniel Pink's September 2010 article about Karl Fisch for the term to stick. Bergmann and Sams are the early pioneers of the flipped movement and both continue to be leaders in education. The "flipped classroom" movement is growing and taking education by storm. The popular TED Talks have now released a Ted Ed website (www.ed.ted.com) designed to share online video lessons and help flip classroom instruction.

### What exactly is a Flipped Classroom?

A flipped classroom refers to actively transferring ownership of learning from the teacher to the student. In-class lectures, often designed using direct instruction pedagogy, are recorded on video and assigned outside of class. The flip occurs when typical project-centered homework, open-ended questions, and guided inquiry instead take place during class time, leveraging the teacher as facilitator and coach rather than lecturer.

The flipped classroom is more than just assigning lecture-style video outside of class. It is about capturing valuable class time with students, increasing student-to-student engagement and teacher-to-student engagement while customizing and personalizing the interactions. It is also about creating a blend of direct instruction, inquiry-based, and constructivist pedagogical approaches.

There is no one, exact "flipped classroom." Rather, there are a handful of choices when considering whether to flip instruction. The first question always remains consistent, "what do my students need to be successful today and in the future?" In the case of Sams and Bergmann their flip involved all students in the class watching lecture-style video as homework which provided increased class time for inquiry-based collaboration, more personalized attention to individual student misconceptions, and a more engaging physical learning environment.

You can see, the flipped classroom is very much in its infancy. While it is exciting on so many fronts and has endless possibilities for education it is important for teachers to be very intentional in their planning choices. This is not about videos and online courses replacing the classroom teacher. It will require skillful instructional design and delivery from today's teachers to blend the right physical (class time) and virtual (outside-of-class time) learning experience for students.

### Blended Learning

Our definition of blended learning comes from Innosight Institute's publication, *The Rise of K–12 Blended Learning,* "Blended learning is any time a student learns in part at a supervised brick and mortar location away from home and at least in part through online delivery with some element of student control over time, place, path, and/or pace." Innosight Institute's report organized and defined the various models of blended learning. These categorizations will help you plan which blended learning methods you'll find most useful.

| Blended Learning Models Adapted from *The Rise of K–12 Blended Learning* | |
|---|---|
| **Face-to-Face Driver** | Most instruction comes from traditional face-to-face with the teacher, but the teacher supplements or remediates instruction with technology in the classroom or computer lab. |
| **Rotation** | Within any given course, the student rotates between online computer-based learning and face-to-face instruction with the teacher. Schedules tend to be fixed but flexible. Classroom teachers monitor the online learning but the learning is self-paced based upon student readiness and mastery of content. |
| **Flex** | Most instruction is delivered on an online platform. Teachers provide as-needed support, in small group settings, and are supplemental instructional support to the online platform. |
| **Online Lab** | Online lab model educational programs are in a brick and mortar online lab with instruction delivered by an online teacher. Paraprofessionals often supervise the computer labs. |
| **Self-Blend** | Students take online courses, where all instruction occurs using teachers in an online platform to supplement their traditional school's face-to-face course catalog. The online learning always occurs remotely, distinguishing it from the Online Lab model. |
| **Online Driver** | Instruction occurs on an online platform, with periodic face-to-face meetings. |

Creating an engaging blended learning classroom environment requires careful consideration to the tasks students complete. The tasks must be *worthwhile* and students must be *meaningfully engaged through interaction with others.* Kearsley and Schneiderman, in "Engagement Theory: A Framework for Technology-Based Teaching and Learning," go on to state:

> *...all student activities involve active cognitive processes such as creating, problem-solving, reasoning, decision-making, and evaluation. In addition, students are intrinsically motivated to learn due to the meaningful nature of the learning environment and activities. Engagement theory is based upon the idea of creating successful collaborative teams that work on ambitious projects that are meaningful to someone outside the classroom. (1999)*

## Multiple Learning Pathways Using Advanced Tools: Social Networks and Anywhere, Anytime Learning

### Early Innovations

As you read earlier in this chapter, web 1.0 solutions assisted users in retrieving vast amounts of information and content which became readily available at the onset of the internet. As such, Learning Object Repositories found their way onto the educational landscape. In researching the history and evolution of **Learning Object Repositories** we found EduTech Wiki (http://edutechwiki.unige.ch/en/Main_Page) a valuable and trusted resource. Learning Object Repositories (LOR) are used by teachers and students alike to digitally store, manage, retrieve, and share digital files used for learning purposes.

As user needs became more sophisticated we saw new and varied systems added to the educational and technology landscape. These systems were in response to specific K–12 needs. Teachers and students would leverage uploading, meta-tagging, and sharing learning objects in different ways. K–12 education sought systems for course management, online learning, and data management that had traditionally been implemented in higher education. **Content Management Systems (CMS)** and **Learning Management Systems (LMS)** became popular solutions both in K–12 education and higher education.

Over the last five years, we have seen many new platforms added to the education space that offer a variety of new options around content and learning management. Content and learning management terms are often used interchangeably and their true definition can be unclear. Sometimes these terms are assigned to a platform that is not a pure CMS or LMS.

In the last few years we have also seen many social media/communication/collaboration platforms arise that have been specifically designed for K–12 education. All of this has created disruptive innovation within the education and technology marketplace. The emergence of new systems that combine various features and have the capacity to extend the learning boundaries by offering customization tools and anytime, anywhere learning continues to grow fast. There is a need within education to name these new, emerging systems. We call these new systems: Digital Learning Systems (DLS).

## The Rise of Digital Learning Systems (DLS)

A digital learning system is an excellent entrance into advanced technology tools that can help you prepare for and organize your students for a blended learning experience. Digital learning systems often provide a range of Web 2.0 and 3.0 functions and combine the most effective features of a LOR, content management system, and learning management system. Our definition of a Digital Learning System is a multi-user, customized learning environment where educators can create, store, reuse, meta-tag, manage, and deliver digital learning content from a central object repository. It allows for the ability to customize instruction through the integration of unique learner profiles and intentional pedagogical choices.

When implementing a DLS in a comprehensive manner, a teacher can:

1. Create an engaging environment around digital content
2. Allow students to create and collaborate online 24/7
3. Streamline and aggregate student data to improve and customize instruction
4. Personalize instructional content and allow for knowledge collection
5. Create an instructional path for students aligned to appropriate standards
6. Consolidate instructional materials on a web-based platform
7. Provide multiple learning pathways in a blended learning environment

Here is a way to think about and understand these terms that we find helpful. The definitions for learning object repository, content management system, and learning management system were retrieved from *EduTech Wiki* on October 2, 2012. The definition of a digital learning system was created by the authors (Smith, Chavez, & Seaman, 2012).

A **learning object repository** is a kind of digital library. It enables educators to share, manage and use educational resources. A more narrow definition would also require that repositories implement a metadata standard.

A **content management system** is a multi-user environment where learning developers can create, store, reuse, manage, and deliver digital learning content from a central object repository.

A **learning management system** (sometimes also called "Course Management System", "Pedagogical Platform", "E-Learning Platform") is a software system that delivers online courses and tutoring.

A **digital learning system** is a multi-user, customized learning environment where educators can create, store, reuse, meta-tag, manage, and deliver digital learning content from a central object repository. It allows for the ability to customize instruction through the integration of unique learner profiles and intentional pedagogical choices.

| | |
|---|---|
| LOR | Static, retrievers of digital content |
| CMS/LMS | Retrievers, creators, and presenters of digital content |
| DLS | Retrievers, creators, customizers, and presenters of digital content |

## Guiding Questions

▶ How do we practically bring the concept of customized 21st century learning into the classroom?

▶ How has technology affected your life in the last ten years?

▶ How has digital content changed the landscape of teaching?

▶ How have you seen technology positively affect teaching and learning? What concerns do you see and wonder about?

## Connecting to Classroom Practice

### Building Customized Classrooms and Fuzzy Logic

Fuzzy logic is a form of reasoning that is approximate and not exact. And while logic might seem more powerful when exact, consider a quote from the 18th century French philosopher Voltaire, *"Le mieux est l'ennemi du bien—*Perfect is the enemy of good," *Dictionnaire Philosophique* (1764). In contrast to traditional logic theory, where binary sets have two values— true or false—fuzzy logic has degrees of truth that range between 0 and 1. Fuzzy logic has been applied to many fields, including artificial intelligence.

Fuzzy logic, like Voltaire's idiom, can be used to customize 21st century learning.

## Making All of this Happen

When dealing with the many moving parts of customizing student learning, consider the difference of completing some of the tasks in front of you to the alternative of *not attempting them at all.* No one is expecting you to customize 21st century learning every minute of your day. One example is formulating the flex networks. While you have many things to consider, including assessment data, student work, and individual student interests and profiles, what is important is not finding the perfect group, but rather creating many opportunities for students to be networked together for many different purposes. In doing so you will foster a rich learning environment that considers a range of possibilities for students. Remember that the perfect is the enemy of good, so don't aim for perfection—aim instead for a practical start at implementing new learning skills in your classroom.

We know that it can be tedious and time consuming to plan customized 21st century learning in your unit and lesson plans. Don't try to do it all at once. Begin by attempting to do a little more than you are doing now—and hopefully you will find some immediate success stories.

In the vignette at the beginning of this chapter, you read about Mr. Sullivan's teaching practice and how it evolved over the course of three years. By the third year, Mr. Sullivan had leveraged his school's digital learning system to flip his classroom instruction. How exactly did he do this?

If 20th century education followed the metaphor of the industrial revolution—an assembly line approach were learning was mass produced and relatively the same, then Mr. Sullivan's 21st century classroom is the opposite. His personalized, customizable learning blueprint was intentionally architected with *each* of his diverse learners in mind.

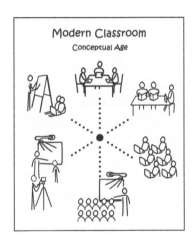

Mr. Sullivan created both physical and virtual learning spaces for his students. His customized classroom had options for whole group teaching which allowed him to utilize many successful teaching strategies with his students. However, it didn't end there. His physical classroom space also had options for small group instruction and peer-to-peer collaboration. These small spaces were designed for several purposes: opportunities for Mr. Sullivan to work directly with a small number of students, opportunities for students to collaborate with each other, opportunities for students to leverage advanced technology tools like the school's digital learning system or other web-enabled applications which effectively and efficiently personalized instruction. He also utilized the school's computer lab, which provided additional blended learning experiences for Mr. Sullivan's students.

The classroom blueprint he designed during his third year teaching seamlessly extended learning outside his physical classroom space. This was made effective because the goals and objectives students were working on were a direct extension to what was happening in the classroom. Unlike traditional after school programs or other web-based educational games, student learning was tightly held together by one integrated classroom blueprint plan that leveraged technology to advance learning goals inside and outside the classroom.

## Creating Digital Playlists—A Place to Begin

Mr. Sullivan began his Egyptian unit of study whole class by asking students to do a quick write. He wanted to know what students already knew about the ancient Egyptians—but he also wanted to assess how his students' writing had progressed since their last writing assignment. He used both pieces of student work to gain a better understanding of the strengths and weaknesses of his whole class and individual students. What he found will not surprise you: a classroom full of diverse learners. In other words, his students' writing was all over the place. How in the world was he going to meet all of their needs? Whole group lessons would quickly lose both his advanced students as well as those students struggling with writing. Even more challenging, he found that some of his advanced students sometimes struggled with one or two discrete writing skills— like when to use a semicolon.

Mr. Sullivan understood that technology was going to help him customize his writing instruction and provide students more time on task by completing these writing mini lessons outside of traditional classroom time. In essence, he was "flipping" his instruction. He was also dispelling a common myth we sometimes hear from teachers, often times stemming from fear, that technology would eventually replace them as the "teacher." In the case of Mr. Sullivan, technology was simply a tool for him to be more effective with his students. Many would argue the role of the teacher is even more important in this scenario.

So Mr. Sullivan set out to create a handful of **digital playlists** of writing mini lessons using a free web-based platform. Each lesson was about 10–15 minutes in length, included Mr. Sullivan's own voice, and provided a set of examples from various writing topics: conventions, spelling, grammar, etc. Mr. Sullivan intentionally selected direct instruction pedagogy. He modeled the examples several times, provided several guided practice problems he wanted students to complete, and built in a quick check for understanding at the end. He was able to upload this digital content into his school's digital learning system, which provided an effective digital hub to organize, store, and present his curriculum.

Now, his newly-created digital playlists allowed him to effectively and efficiently meet a classroom full of students' diverse needs in writing. The playlists allowed students to pause the lesson as needed, which allowed the student to vary the pacing based on their own learning preferences and needs at that moment. The option to replay the playlist allowed students to go back and watch Mr. Sullivan's modeling for a second or third time, or skip over parts of the lesson once they understood it. He also created a handful of visuals within each lesson, which helped his visual learners organize and understand the content. He was also able to find a free translation service online which benefited one student in his class whose primary language was Créole. This student could view the playlist in both his primary language and in English creating a unique learning opportunity for the content and his language development.

The digital learning system that Mr. Sullivan used includes a customized media player, equipped with a host of functions that Mr. Sullivan leveraged instructionally.

Mr. Sullivan taught his class how to access the Digital Learning System from any internet-connected device. He also taught them how to use the functions of the media player to assist them in their learning. Media players vary depending on the system being used. Mr. Sullivan was lucky to have a host of options to share with his students: volume control, varied audio speed options, action buttons: play, pause, rewind , closed captioning, additional languages, full-screen viewing. He also took advantage of the options to segment video and select customized content for his playlist. His digital learning system allowed him to segment and customize both the video he created and uploaded as well as video he had found within the system.

Mr. Sullivan assigned these writing mini lessons throughout his unit of study, sometimes only assigning one or two students each night—and would then follow up with each student the next day during independent and collaborative work time. Assigning only a handful of playlists each night made follow-up a bit more manageable. He found that he needed a little longer with each student in follow-up because the content was writing. At other times he was able to assign the entire class playlists, but that depended on the content.

**Playlist** is *a customized collection of **digital content** for future playback.* Playlists become instructional when it is annotated to support your specific lesson, is intentionally aligned to a specific pedagogy, and has been designed to support the customization of learning in the classroom.

**Digital Content** is video, video segments, audio, images, interactive whiteboard files, screen captures, interactive files, *e*books, web links, power points, or any other digital asset.

### Playlist Design and Instructional Intent

Digital Learning Playlists can be used in a variety of ways to meet the learning needs of a classroom and individual students. Playlists can be viewed outside of the classroom, or at home, as well as inside the classroom whole group or in small groups; the options are endless. The options selected for using and viewing playlists should align with the customizing needs of the classroom and individual students. Here are some ways we have used and observed teachers using playlists:

**Playlists can be used to:**

▶ Introduce a lesson

▶ Teach the same content with varied pedagogical approaches

▶ Review or reinforce content

▶ Teach mini lessons

▶ Re-teach content

▶ Preview content

▶ Extend learning beyond core standards and content

▶ Absentee playlist

▶ Teach flipped classroom lessons

Mr. Sullivan used both in-class time and outside class time to teach writing. Students would often collaborate together—using the small group spaces in the classroom—proof reading each other's writing and offering up suggestions. The school's computer lab was used to type up their writing or research content, and the school's digital learning system was used both in class and outside of class for mini lessons. Mr. Sullivan was able to customize his instruction based upon his students' academic readiness, interests, intelligence preferences, culture, language, and sometimes gender. By using technology and research-based teaching methods Mr. Sullivan provides for us a vision of 21st century instructional design and delivery.

### Student Choice: Invite them into the Process

One of the most powerful ways to accelerate student achievement is to invest them in their own learning. One way is to share on-going assessment results with students while asking them to think about their own learning. While this typically happens during parent-teacher conferences, it is more powerful if it's embedded into classroom routines. During one-on-one student time, ask them about their interests and follow up with opportunities to share these interests. Look for signs of student learning styles and preferences. Simply asking if they prefer working at a desk or moving around, alone or in groups, can go a long way towards student learning customization. You can use this information when building unit or lesson plans.

Alternately, you may want to ask students about their learning relative to a few specific standards. Having students describe their understanding of a particular concept will help determine content misconceptions. This information is helpful when creating flexible groupings, re-teaching groups, or when differentiating for students.

Student choice can happen in a number of other ways as well. As discussed earlier, another strategy for engaging students is to provide choice in the learning product. Having students engaged in authentic tasks could result in students creating and publishing their own digital content from a myriad of choices involving web 2.0 tools. Refer to the list of 2.0 technology tools for additional options.

## Blueprint Essentials

Education is ready to move away from an industrial model of education to a more modern classroom. This shift requires teachers to design both physical and virtual learning spaces for students.

The modern classroom is customized based upon each student's learner profile. A learner profile considers a student's learning style, intelligence preferences, culture, gender, academic readiness, and interests before planning and designing instruction.

The modern classroom also understands and knows the 21st century learner. These learners were born digital and will require new skills to compete in the global economy.

The modern classroom also embraces technology and should be leveraged to customize the classroom experience and provide additional learning pathways beyond the traditional classroom.

## Reflection and Action

### Reflection

▶ What are you left thinking about?

▶ What questions do you have about Mr. Sullivan's classroom?

▶ What questions do you have about technology?

### Action

▶ What one or two things can you do today to customize your teaching?

▶ What technology can you leverage to assist you?

# In the Library

## Differentiation

*How to Differentiate Instruction
in Mixed Ability Classrooms* (2004)
Carol Ann Tomlinson

*Differentiation and the Brain: How Neuroscience
Supports the Learner-Friendly Classroom* (2010)
Carol Ann Tomlinson, David Sousa

## Technology and Innovation

*Flip Your Classroom* (2012)
Jonathon Bergmann, Aaron Sams

*What School Leaders Need to Know About
Digital Technologies and Social Media* (2012)
Scott McLeod, Chris Lehmann

*Disrupting Class: How Disruptive Innovation
Will Change the Way the World Learns* (2008)
Clayton Christensen

# Journal Entry

**Virtual Teacher Architect**
**Date:** It's your turn. Build your virtual re-imaged classroom. Take the time to visit http://classroom.4teachers.org and bring your blueprint to life by designing the optimal learning space for your students. How does this image compare to the picture you took of your classroom in Chapter 1? What one or two things can you do tomorrow to move closer to your ideal image? Record your thoughts here.

**Experiencing and Personalizing your Journey**

Challenge yourself to re-imagine your classroom from some of the key concepts from this chapter. What does it look like? What core principles from this book are evident in the new design of your physical and virtual learning space?

Recently, I took a trip to the famous Water Tower Place on Chicago's Magnificent Mile and visited the Lego store. Immediately, ideas from my childhood returned. The store was filled with children and adults—all experiencing a sense of what could be created. In my opportunity to re-imagine what could be I was filled with a sense of wonder, amazement, possibility, and intrigue.

# Chapter 7

# Instructional Materials
## and the
## 21st Century

# A Teacher's Story: New Instructional Materials

*Trevor, a third grade teacher in Minnesota, spotted a box on his desk as he walked into his classroom. He smiled slightly, relieved and excited; glad the eight-month process of selecting the school's new math series was complete. It had been exhausting but as he opened the box could almost feel the energy packed up in it.*

*Then he saw on the floor next to his desk two stacked piles—seven more boxes waiting for him. He'd heard teachers' concerns that the instructional materials would be overwhelming, that the pedagogy and teaching methods were new, and some feared that the consumables seemed to lack the rigor needed for kids to be successful with the state's new standards. He sat down at his desk and murmured, "How in the world are we ever going to implement this?" Just then he heard the announcement over the intercom, "Third through fifth grade teachers, your math workshop is starting in five minutes in the library." He sighed, thinking: It can only get better.*

## Connect and Reflect

### What is Alignment?

Because **alignment** means many different things within the educational system, we want to be specific when discussing instructional alignment. According to the *Merriam Webster Dictionary*, alignment is defined as the "proper positioning or state of adjustment of the parts in relationship to each other." In instructional design, we align to make our teaching practice more efficient and effective. In education, alignment is deliberately integrating smooth and helpful connections between all the parts of our work—lectures, conferencing, planning, recordkeeping, encouraging, assessing—all of it.

The **parts** we consider for alignment are: standards, Cognitive Growth Targets, assessments, instructional materials, instructional cycles, curriculum maps, units, lessons, student objectives/goals, pedagogy, and high-impact teaching behaviors. The key to alignment is how we integrate the core functions of each part; we must seek to connect everything to learning outcomes. This happens when we intentionally design processes in which one part of our work deeply affects another part. The architect or designer, the **teacher**—you—put it all together.

## Putting the Parts Together

A common understanding and definition of the parts and alignment considerations helps us move towards building your classroom instructional blueprint.

▶ **Standards:** Standards define what we want students to know (content) and be able to do (skills) within a continuum of kindergarten through grade 12. They are most commonly grouped by grade level and are determined through state and district adoptions. The Common Core State Standards in English Language Arts and Mathematics are an option for all states to adopt a new evolution of shared standards across the United States. To date, 46 states have adopted the Common Core.

▶ **Cognitive Growth Targets:** An organized target of the thinking processes that promote student learning and thinking. The purpose of the Cognitive Growth Targets is to intentionally design tasks and activities that span the targets, with particular attention towards movement inward. 21st century instruction deeply depends on the teacher's ability to design opportunities for student thinking that utilizes analysis, reasoning, and creation. The Growth Targets are the lens through which we organize and design 21st century classrooms.

▶ **Assessment:** A process by which we determine a student's progress towards meeting instructional goals or standards. There are many options and formats for assessments. Due to the diversity of students, we recommend a variety of assessments (e.g., classroom observation, constructed response, selected response, and performance assessment).

▶ **Curriculum Mapping:** A process by which teachers record the standards and content taught and how they will/have assessed them. Maps are shared and examined across grade levels, schools, and districts for coherency and alignment and this involves the ongoing communication of all stakeholders in the curriculum. Maps can include information such as instructional cycles, instructional materials, higher-order thinking alignment, and student tasks and activities. Map content beyond standards and assessment can vary across districts and is generally connected to unit and lesson planning procedures.

▶ **Instructional Cycles:** Unit of time used to organize instructional content over the school year. Cycles are generally aligned to school calendar or school and district assessment calendars (e.g., 10 week/semester; 13 week/trimester; 5–6 week/aligned to assessments). Instructional cycles vary among districts and schools.

▶ **Instructional Materials:** Any materials used to teach students, including text, books, visuals, manipulatives, 3D models, digital content, etc.

▶ **Digital Media/Digital Content/Digital Assets:** Digital media, digital assets, and digital content—anything available in digital form that can be opened and viewed on a computer or digital display. This includes video, audio, documents, interactive documents, eBooks, weblinks, and more. Education today can take just about any instructional material and make it digital. 21st century teaching requires regular integrated use of digital content.

▶ **Pedagogy:** Pedagogy is the way in which you build learning within a lesson: the order of and the specific steps or elements of the lesson that will be used to build/scaffold/create the learning experience for students. There are a variety of pedagogical approaches for lesson planning. (Chapter 8 explores specific steps and templates for the Direct Instruction, Constructivist, and Inquiry-Based pedagogies.) Pedagogy should be varied within a unit plan and chosen based on the best learning plan for each specific lesson's goals and individual/group of students' needs. Good architects of learning use a variety of pedagogical choices because no one approach is the best for all plans and lessons. There are benefits to allowing students to think and learn in different ways and to not always build the learning the same way for all lessons.

▶ **Units of Study:** A unit plan is a series of lessons organized around a theme or topic and an identified set of standards. The unit plan defines an instructional time frame from a few days, to a week, or up to several weeks depending on the content and the instructional cycles that are in place. The unit plan takes the year-long curriculum map big picture and provides more specifics for the identified time frame. A unit map will generally include the year-long curriculum map information in more detail and adds in the following details: theme, big ideas, essential questions, standards breakdown, student objectives, academic vocabulary, student ownership, parent connections, alignment planning for rigor, and pedagogical choices.

▶ **Lesson Plans:** A lesson plan defines the specific action plan the teacher will take to teach the standard(s). A lesson plan generally occurs within a single day and a specified amount of time. It is possible for a lesson to extend over more days. A lesson plan articulates the desired learning outcomes (standards), the pedagogical choice, instructional strategies, questioning strategies, tasks and activities, assessments, rubrics, and all detailed steps for teaching, facilitating, and implementing the lesson effectively.

▶ **Instructional Strategies:** Instructional choices that support the pedagogy, thinking, and learning goals selected for the lesson. Instructional strategies assist in setting up the learning experience students will go through during the lesson.

▶ **Student/Unit/Lesson Objective(s):** Statement about what a student will be able to demonstrate as a result of experiencing that unit or lesson. Unit objectives apply to the completion of all lessons in the unit. Lesson objectives are specific outcomes for that individual lesson. The standards serve this purpose often, but sometimes it becomes necessary to break down objectives to meet the whole of the standard.

▶ **21st Century Differentiation:** Customizing student learning based upon each student's learning profile: their academic readiness, interests, learning styles, intelligence preferences, culture, and gender to create an academic environment that is mobile, adaptive, and flexible to meet the needs of 21st century learners. Begin by creating learner profiles in your classroom and then leverage advanced technology tools to make 21st century differentiation more efficient and effective. 21st century differentiation is described in detail in Chapter 6: Customizing and Enriching Student Learning.

▶ **Re-Teaching:** Process by which teachers monitor progress throughout the unit and at the end of the unit for student mastery of standards. Data is used to organize re-teach opportunities during and following the completion of a unit of study.

▶ **High-Impact Teaching (HIT) Behaviors:** Specific teaching behaviors that have a positive correlation (causal relationship) with student achievement. We detail HIT behaviors in Chapter 9.

*A common understanding and set of terms around lesson design as we move forward through our plan will be helpful. What terms and common language do you and your colleagues use to discuss lesson design? Establishing a local glossary of professional terms can foster collaboration and a strong learning community.*

Let's explore the history and evolution of instructional materials within public education—in other words, what is our inherited background of all these parts? How instructional materials have evolved within public education has led us to the exciting new options digital content and technology offer today's classrooms.

# Why We Do What We Do

## History of Instructional Materials in America

While Chapter 1 looked at the history and development of standards in education, this chapter reveals the history of instructional materials, the first text books, and the role they played in the development of American ideas about learning. The same **ask** that drives schools and teachers to change, drives the educational publishing industry as well.

The first public school in 1635 focused on teaching children how to be good citizens and read and understand the Bible. It can be said that the first *unofficial* text book in public schools was the Bible. Colonial schools also used hornbooks for instructional and study material. Hornbooks originated in England in the 1450s and while the term has been applied to a variety of study materials in different fields, it is simply a piece of wood with words printed on both sides. In early childhood education, hornbooks consisted of a leaf, vellum, or paper sheet with the alphabet, then vowels, then Roman numerals, and lastly the Lord's Prayer. It was affixed to a wooden board with a handle, and a sheet of transparent cow horn covered the board for protection. Students would hold it up in front of them by the handle to study the material. The handle was also designed to hang from a child's belt. A hornbook always had a large cross at the top, usually carved in the wood and was often called your Christ Cross Row or criss-cross-row.

Initially, schoolbooks were brought over from England for use in American schools. The *English Protestant Tutor* was a popular schoolbook but Boston publishers reprinted it in 1690 under the title *The New England Primer*. With its additional material and American updates, it became one of the most widely-used text books in 18th century public schools. It was quickly not without competition, and the textbook industry in America was born.

## Webster and American English

As a schoolmaster in the 18th century, Noah Webster was frustrated that the only textbooks available were from England. Webster was an educator, an editor, a political visionary, a writer, and a publisher. He felt American students should learn from American books. He wrote and published A *Grammatical Institute of the English Language*, in three volumes: a Speller (1783), a Grammar (1784), and a Reader (1785). Webster, breaking from traditional Puritan-driven predecessors, infused American lifestyle and language into his books, asserting that grammar and pronunciation from England and America needed to be distinguished. He felt that the British had corrupted the English language and rejected the notion that children must study Greek and Latin before learning English. He was known as a spelling reformer, changing the spelling of traditional British English into American English, simplifying rules and adding words used only in America.

The speller became widely used and was called the *Blue-Backed Speller* because of its blue cover. It was organized by increasing complexity, progressing by student's age and ability, predating Jean Piaget's theory of cognitive development. It became the most popular American book of its time, selling 60 million copies by 1890. For 100 years, it taught students how to read, spell, and pronounce words and even gave rise to the concept of the Spelling Bee. It was also historically significant in that it was completely secular, a first for textbooks.

Webster today is known for his dictionaries. First published in 1806, his dictionary evolved over his lifetime and several editions were published as the language changed.

## A New Generation of Readers

The 19th century provoked the next generation of school books. In 1833, a small publishing company in Cincinnati saw a relatively open market for text books and looked for an educator to write them. They commissioned William McGuffey, an Oxford professor, to create a reading series. McGuffey produced four readers and his brother the fifth and sixth volumes. They were originally called *Eclectic Readers* as they represented varied sources, opinions, and topics.

McGuffey also produced a teacher's guide to accompany his readers, and this was an important model for what text books have become today. McGuffey's personal philosophies on American life were reflected in his books and influenced a century of American children. McGuffey's name was later added to the title and this series became more influential in American culture than any other of its time other than the Bible.

The first American-published mathematics text for elementary schools, *The New and Complete System of Arithmetic*, was written by Nicholas Pike, a New Hampshire native and graduate of Harvard. Pike's work was recognized by the presidents and professors of the leading colleges of the time and is considered a significant influence on education and the study of mathematics.

After its publication in 1786, George Washington wrote a letter to Pike stating that, "The handsome manner in which that Work is printed and the elegant manner in which it is bound, are pleasing proofs of the progress which the Arts are making in this Country." It was seen as progress for our nation and economy because an American-written and published math text meant the colonies no longer had to depend on British publications.

*Pike's Arithmetic,* as it was called, remained the prominent elementary school math text book into the early 1800s and went through many revisions and reprinting.

This book is part of the author's rare book collection and we draw inspiration from this and others in the collection, knowing that many

**Figure 7.1 –** *is a first edition, first printing of Pike's The New and Complete System of Arithmetic.*

before us have spent a lifetime pursuing the same work we pursue today—educating our nation's youth.

## Historical Perspective: Then and Now

Over time, the need for and production of books and instructional materials grew into all of the core subjects and beyond. The need was again driven by society's trends and what the political climate called for within education. Today, text book and instructional material legislation surfaced with the onset of NCLB. To maintain federal funding sources, states had to establish compliance laws for instructional materials. Such laws vary state to state and cover everything from accessibility, cost, size, weight, and digital content options. Meeting special student population needs and the demand for digital content and technology integration are a new **ask** of the education publishing industry. The **ask** of public education and so the **ask** of instructional materials to meet the needs of learners evolves every day.

## Instructional Materials and the 21st Century

It's only a decade into the 21st century and we can easily say that the classroom and its instructional materials already look very different than they did in 2000. What kind of classroom and instructional materials do we need to teach tomorrow's students?

The current movement in the publishing of instructional materials is being driven by the Common Core State Standards and technology. For the first time in the history of public education, 90% of the United States will be operating with the same standards. This changes the business for publishers who no longer must align their materials to 50 different state-adopted standards. It is our hope that the simplification and unification of what constitutes learning in America will free up the industry to provide high-quality, clearly-aligned materials with pedagogy and activities for 21st century learning.

In Chapter 6, we explored the 21st century classroom, digital media, and the blended learning model. Again, let's consider what it means to be a 21st century learner.

## Guiding Questions

▶ What will the world look like in 2030? What will the societal and economical needs be?

▶ What kind of jobs will my students be seeking in 2030?

▶ How will my classroom today begin to prepare my students for future success?

# Connecting to Classroom Practice

In 2030, today's kindergarteners will graduate from college and compete for jobs. We have seen through this book's journey how the world and society in America has changed and influenced public education for the last 300 years. Just the last five years has shown significant change in how our global society and economy functions and communicates. These changes affect overall trends and have an impact on every household and job in America.

Although much has been written about 21st century skills in education over the last decade, the concept has really only recently become popular. The Conceptual Age requires students to learn new skill sets in addition to a new application of old skill sets. 21st century skills are not only about technology but are about what we need to teach students to successfully communicate and function in today's world and to be able to adapt to the demands of tomorrow's jobs. Technology affects the learning pathways in which students access content, how we teach, opportunities for differentiation, and how we communicate.

The Partnership for the 21st Century Skills, a national organization that advocates for 21st century readiness for every student, *(Trilling and Fadel 2009)* defines these skills as follows (as previously seen in chapter 6):

**Learning and Innovation Skills**

▶ Creativity and Innovation

▶ Critical Thinking and Problem Solving

▶ Communication and Collaboration

**Digital Literacy Skills**

▶ Information Literacy

▶ Media Literacy

▶ Information and Communication Literacy

**Career and Life Skills**

▶ Flexibility and Adaptability

▶ Initiative and Self-Direction

▶ Social and Cross-Cultural Skills

▶ Productivity and Accountability

▶ Leadership and Responsibility

As you read in Chapter 2, the Cognitive Growth Targets align with and are structured to create 21st century thinkers. We encourage you to read more about 21st century skills as they are essential specifications in the instructional design process. These skills provide a framework that defines and guides teaching and learning for today's classrooms.

## Digital Textbooks?

In early 2012, at New York City's Guggenheim museum, Apple announced it was going to "reinvent the textbook" with its plans to launch e-textbooks. With over 1.5 million iPads used in education in early 2012 and more than 20,000 education-related apps, Apple's announcement had a big effect on education's publishing industry. Apple plans to initially partner with the big three of educational textbook publishing that are responsible for over 90% of industry sales, although there are still many details that need to be worked out.

The new e-textbook will feature 3D-animated models of academic content, video access, and written content—all without leaving the page. The content will be constantly updated, making the information relevant and real-time. The e-textbook will have built-in features like quizzes, and post-its that allow students to make text annotations with the ability to aggregate them into virtual note cards. What implications will e-books have for 21st century teachers? Will this become status quo for 21st century students?

## Evaluative Criteria for Instructional Materials

You make decisions every day about what instructional materials you will use: text books, trade books, guided reading books, supplemental books, visuals, posters, models, digital content, video, images, pictures, manipulatives— anything you use to teach. A thoughtful analysis of the textbooks and programs you are considering and/or must use will give you a better understanding of the materials and how they can be best used to support learning in your classroom. Consider the following:

**Content:** Which standards and learning goals or objectives are specifically identified in the instructional materials?

**Assessments:** What formal and informal assessments are provided and embedded in the materials?

> *The instructional materials we choose and use greatly affect the teaching and learning in our classrooms. We push you to ask what types of instructional materials you regularly use— and which materials do you rarely or never use? How could adding them to your plan affect learning for your students?*

**Structures and Organization/Presentation:** How are the materials organized? How do they present material to students? What is the conceptual organization?

**Motivation and Reinforcement:** What opportunities for reinforcement and support are built-in?

**Reading Level:** What is the reading level of student materials? Are there options within the instructional materials for varied reading levels?

**Instructional Analysis:** What pedagogies, if any, are built into the instructional materials? How are concepts introduced and built within the instructional materials? Academic vocabulary? Options for differentiation? Supplemental and special population support materials (ELL, Gifted, Special Education, etc.)?

**Rigor:** Use the Cognitive Growth Targets to identify rigor within the materials. What activities and tasks are provided for students?

**Digital Content:** Do the instructional materials provide digital content for both teacher and student?

**Technology:** Do the instructional materials embed technology links and use in the instructional material?

**21st Century Skills:** How does the text support developing 21st century skills for students?

This is a basic list of components and considerations to help frame questions as you review and evaluate instructional materials for your classroom.

When grade levels, schools, or districts adopt new materials, they engage in a formal process and typically develop a set of criteria they are looking for and a rubric for evaluating the materials. When selecting instructional materials, teachers must be as intentional about choices and align them to students' needs and unit and lesson plans. Use a variety of instructional materials to meet the needs of diverse learners.

## From Design to Build

Alignment, designing connections between all the parts of our work, makes our teaching more effective. The key is to connect alignment to learning outcomes. Our role is to design the parts of classroom instruction into a coherent blueprint. Chapters 1–5 discussed all of the parts in education that fulfill Core Principle 1: Designing with Purpose—and 6 & 7 discussed Core Principle 2: Customizing 21st Century Learning—by refining this design for the next generation of learners.

Now, your job is to bring connectivity to these isolated parts by drawing out the distinctive concepts and integrating them together. This is your practice—a well thought-out instructional blueprint aimed at ensuring academic, social, and emotional growth for each student you teach—built into a successful classroom environment. Chapter 8 concludes the planning of our design for more effective teaching as it pulls all the parts together with tools and templates to make your planning more efficient.

## Blueprint Essentials

While the Standards and school-mandated materials can be overwhelming, you can empower yourself by knowledgeably and strategically using them to support the learning in your classroom.

Alignment is the process of intentionally and purposefully making all the parts work together.

Seek to select instructional materials that create the thinking and experiences that students need to meet the demands of 21st century learning.

Be aware of the many parts that come together to build instruction in your classroom, how they fit together, and the power of each decision you make for your students.

## In the Library

### Preparing for New Skills

*21st Century Skills Learning for Life in Our Times* (2009)
Bernie Trilling and Charles Fadel

*Curriculum 21 Essential Education for a Changing World* (2010)
Heidi Hayes Jacobs, ASCD

*The Partnership for 21st Century Skills*
(http://www.21stcenturyskills.org)

*Teaching 21st Century Skills* (2011)
Sue Beers

# Reflection and Action

## Reflection

▶ What instructional materials do you currently use in your classroom?

▶ Which ones are mandated by your school or district?

▶ Which ones did you select on your own?

▶ How well do your instructional materials assist in addressing 21st Century Skills?

▶ Do you have digital content available and how often do you use digital media to teach your students?

## Action

▶ Use the Evaluative Criteria for Instructional Materials from this chapter to perform an initial analysis of the materials you currently use.

▶ Seek ways to incorporate digital content into your classroom.

▶ Seek to understand the professional language of your school and district—how do they define the parts, elements or pieces of the instructional process?

# Journal Entry

**Experiencing and Personalizing your Journey**

**Mind Mapping:** There are many parts to designing highly-effective teaching.

How are you thinking about the relationship of these parts?

Using the terms from Chapters 1–7 make a sketch that shows how you think about these parts and their relationship to each other.

# Chapter 8

# Designing
## Classroom Instruction:
## The Blueprint

# A Teacher's Story: Putting It All Together

*"Honey, I'm home.
How was teacher institute day?"*

*"It went well. My principal said that to plan effective instruction,
it's as simple as using **all** of these things..."*

## Connect and Reflect

As a new teacher or a veteran, we've all been there…we have all this stuff to use for planning and the questions begin: Where do I start? What do I use? What is ok not to use? How do these make sense together? Do I have enough time to do this right? What is *most* important?

Along this journey we've discussed many of the building blocks that go into instructional design along with the theory, research, and best practices that guide us. Now, it's time to put it all together.

# Why We Do What We Do

So far, this book has stepped you through procedures and goals you are already familiar with, but in a different way. Approaching the calling of teaching as an architect of instruction means stepping back a bit to view just how you are putting together all the parts of your learning plan. You are building the blueprint for your classroom: first get the specs, then design, then test, then build.

In Chapter 1, we learned about standards reform and how we determine what students should know and be able to do. Chapter 2 connected the importance of higher-order thinking and introduced you to the Cognitive Growth Targets. Chapter 3 detailed how to breakdown and work with the new Common Core State Standards. Next, Chapter 4 explored the types of assessments and their varied purposes for documenting learning. Chapter 5 explained how the brain processes and learns, explained the most relevant learning theories in K–12 classrooms, and demonstrated how to fine-tune the learning process with pedagogical approaches and instructional strategies. Chapter 6 connected 21st Century Skills to customized teaching and learning. Chapter 7 explored instructional materials, summarized and defined a set of terms that we use across this book to discuss teaching, and illustrated how alignment is a tool for effective planning. All of these pieces come together in the **Instructional Design Process**.

## The History of Mapping and Instructional Design

Before we put it all together, let's take a look at the purpose and history of K–12 curriculum mapping and unit planning. Fenwick W. English is considered the father of curriculum management audits and mapping. A graduate of the University of Southern California, he began his career as a third grade teacher in Los Angeles in the late 1960s and continues to influence and challenge education policies and practices today. He believed that quality curriculum and accountability were essential for a successful education system. He pushed curriculum audit and mapping reform needs to the surface in the early 1980s. He is currently president of an education company that supports curriculum mapping.

## Curriculum Mapping and Purpose

Curriculum mapping is a process by which all teachers plan for and then record the standards and content they have taught and how they have assessed them. Maps tell us what to teach and when.

Heidi Hayes Jacobs is a leader in curriculum mapping. Her curriculum mapping model is adapted and used all over the world. Like English, her work began in the 1980s and has evolved over the decades. Dr. Jacobs has added to the work of English with her own defined content and process for mapping. She expanded initial thoughts on mapping to include horizontal and vertical alignment, cyclic reviews, and curricular dialogue among teachers and administrators. Jacobs' model has led to a common practice of mapping to guide teaching and learning decisions across education. Jacobs stressed the importance of communication taking place between teachers and across grade levels—the maps themselves and their particular format were of less importance. Jacobs states that a variety of models can be effective but that they all must include ongoing dialogue.

Fellow educators Janet Hale and Susan Udelhofen have published books that are widely used to guide the curriculum mapping process. These authors support the same values around the purpose and need for mapping; each provides a different set of tools and a lens, but they all agree that the process is essential and that mapping is never "done" but is an ongoing and collaborative process. We agree: a cohesive, high-quality curriculum needs mapping and collaboration.

Ideally, maps are shared and examined across grade levels, schools, and districts for coherency and alignment. Mapping is a process involving the ongoing communication of all curriculum stakeholders. Maps can include information such as: instructional cycles, instructional materials, higher-order thinking alignment, student tasks, and activities. Map content beyond standards and assessment can vary across districts and is generally dependent upon the process in place for unit and lesson planning.

Mapping tools are evolving every day. Online collaboration opportunities for teachers to share, interact, and be reflective are changing the landscape of curriculum mapping. We believe mapping options will continue to grow and provide new and innovative ways to plan and align instruction. It is essential to have a big picture map that begins with standards and assessment planning—how it looks and how it is shared and reflected upon over the school year can vary. The important thing is that it is happening and that teachers are engaged in the process together.

Why do we map?

▶ You need a plan

▶ Program coherency

▶ Standards, 21st century skills, and higher-order thinking alignment

▶ Promotes reflective inquiry and collaboration

▶ Creates an understanding of student learning/thinking within the curriculum

**Mapping in Practice**

*We have found out in the field that typically, a variety of types of maps and processes are used. Any set of steps and templates can be used to map, as long as you are achieving the goals set forth for mapping and you are creating useful documents to guide teaching and learning. We find that most schools use grade level or school year-long maps aligned to core instructional materials. Most often, core text books are driving the mapping process for schools and districts. Yet clear documentation or understanding of how they are used and aligned to classroom teaching and learning is generally varied or non-existent. Teachers often have **Plan Books** vs. **Diary Maps** and the level to which individual teachers are reflecting after teaching is varied. Most teachers or schools engage in the processes of mapping but not always in a school-wide, strategic or cohesive way. Some districts and schools have comprehensive mapping practices and structured collaboration time.*

*We encourage you to engage in the process your district practices and to strive for collaboration and ongoing dialogue with your colleagues about what you are teaching and the experiences and thinking that you want students to engage in over the school year.*

The four recognized Curriculum Map types are the Essential Map, Consensus Map, Projected Map, and Diary Map.

**Essential Map**—District-wide map created collaboratively to outline by month the learning expectations for each content area based on standards and frameworks.

**Consensus Map**—School site map created collaboratively by school site staff that outlines the learning expectations for each content area based on standards and frameworks. Consensus maps are specific to school-site instructional materials and resources. Consensus maps ensure alignment of standards and assessments.

**Projected Map**—Teacher-level planning based on Consensus Map.

**Diary Map**—After instruction, teachers record what was actually taught and reflect on the instruction. These notes are used for future planning and to modify instruction and maps as the school year progresses.

## Unit Planning and Lesson Planning

Unit Planning and Lesson Planning have existed individually throughout the history of education. The two come into the design process once the big picture mapping is laid out for the school year. As you read in Chapter 5, there are many pedagogical approaches to lesson planning. Lesson planning or lesson plans refer to the specific description for a single lesson or day. Planning a unit of study generally means content and student objectives to be taught over a particular period and/or within a specific theme.

Over the last decade, the concept and purpose of Unit Planning evolved with the work of Wiggins and McTighe's book, *Understanding by Design.* Their emphasis is on "backward design," the practice of looking at the learning outcomes to design curriculum units that emphasize teaching for learning. The principles in this nationally-recognized work detail the unit planning process.

*It takes time to develop maps, unit plans and lesson plans. You may not have every piece clear and documented as you embark on teaching each year, and that is to be expected and part of the process. Begin with the basics, add to your maps and plans as you go, and build your skills and learning to adapt and customize to your individual student needs year by year.*

Much is published about unit design, and many education templates are available. And while much has been written about mapping, and unit and lesson planning, each component is typically written about in isolation and no educational resource seems to put it all together. As you read on, *Teacher as Architect* outlines the process for instructional design and tools to unite the parts.

## Teacher As Architect Instructional Design

The *instructional design process* is a journey you'll be on throughout your career. You will learn and refine every year—as the world changes, as you change—and as society's **ask** and student needs change. We know it's complicated. And while there is importance to the complexity of planning and teaching, there is often unnecessary complication to the process. For instance, the many tools to assist in instructional design often focus on only **one** very specific element of the process, and there are so many elements to work with and put together. Educational resources can tend to feel scattered and disconnected—leaving teachers to wonder: *How do I put this all together?*

Whether you are joining the TAA journey in teacher pre-service, as a new teacher, or a skilled veteran, remember that it is a process in which you grow and we encourage you to take on one part at a time. Teacher as Architect will support you in your planning, delivery, and reflection of your craft and seek to make a very complex process efficient, effective, and connected.

*As educators, each step, piece and part that we do in our field is complex and deeply personal— its importance rooted in each child's needs and the future of our world. Few, if any, other professions have such responsibilities.*

*Our approach to building instruction is rooted in teachers understanding best practices, having a structure and knowing the important details necessary for instructional design and delivery in the 21st century.*

## Planning with 21st Century Tools

Currently, our profession has access to online tools to curriculum map as well as a variety of share files or DLS options for sharing unit plans, lesson plans, and instructional documents. Your district may even have an option (or expectation) of collaboration and sharing of teaching materials. How have these 21st century technology tools affected your teacher planning and teaching? Have they helped? What's missing? Because what we have not found in the teacher resource market is software that helps you design and build your unit plans and lesson plans based on best practices and teaching effectiveness.

Teacher as Architect is developing software to automate the completion of the instructional design templates and to guide your planning process. These templates link vital resources and information to make planning quicker and easier—while building in learning theory and pedagogical choices. We realize that teachers need to have the right "stuff" all in one place for planning and teaching and that we need to make it efficient and effective for you. As you evolve and become experts in specific elements of instruction, we aim to provide ongoing support. Our Blueprint series of books and workbooks, each with a specific focus on a design component and its elements, will further guide instructional design and delivery. You will also have the opportunity to join the Teacher as Architect Online Community where you can research, reference, and share ideas.

## Guiding Questions

▶ What are the components I need to build a Classroom Blueprint? What information do I need? Where do I begin?

▶ How do I stay on track and monitor my thinking around planning?

▶ What is the relationship between daily lessons, units of study and year-long planning?

▶ How do I reflect and refine my plans throughout the year and the teaching journey?

▶ How can I connect the parts of planning into a coherent blueprint? How will I align all of the vital parts of the plan?

▶ Complexity and Simplicity: What are the most important parts to the blueprint that will deliver success for each student in my class?

## Connecting to Classroom Practice

### The Planning Process: Intention and Reflection

The planning process is complex and multi-layered, but with a clear framework and understanding of what is important, teachers can efficiently design a plan for student success. Our journey has attempted to lay the foundation with the design components and elements necessary to build your classroom blueprint.

One of the lessons we have learned over the years is that successful teachers are intentional about their instructional choices and that they plan diligently at every level for the teaching and learning process.

## The Components of Instructional Design

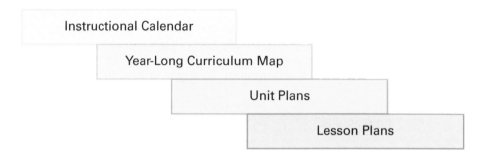

### Instructional Calendar

Initiating the instructional design process starts with your instructional calendar, which begins by plotting the dates you will administer mandated local and state assessments to your students. Include grading periods and other instructional impacts on the calendar for the school year and build in any common interim assessments established by your grade level team, school site, district, and or state. This calendar will assist you as you create your year-long map. For detailed steps to creating an instructional calendar, please refer to Chapter 4.

### Year-Long Curriculum Mapping

The year-long template is a document that any teacher can use to establish the basic elements of an essential year-long plan. Be aware of the expectations around mapping and collaboration at your school and engage in that process. Mapping can be done by a single teacher for their classroom plan, by grade level teams, or across a school site or district. We encourage and support collaboration across all levels of the system; without coherent communication across the system, we cannot do our best work. While we acknowledge that not all schools have systems in place to support curriculum and planning collaboration, every teacher, regardless of current school leadership around mapping, begins with the big picture and plans for learning in their classroom.

TAA Year-Long Mapping Template:

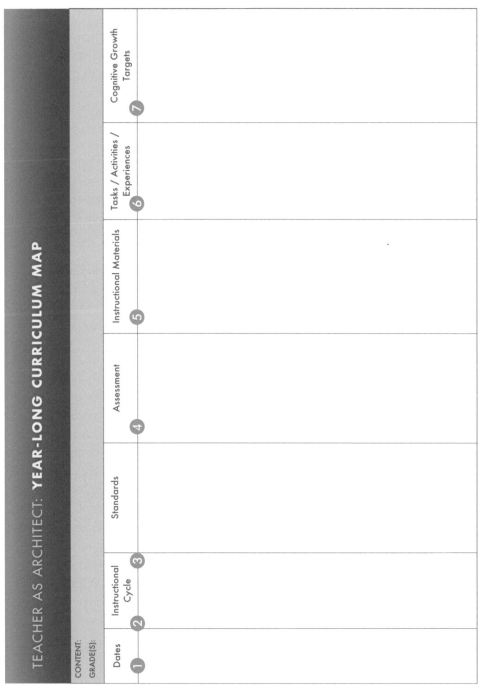

## Using the TAA Year-Long Mapping Template:

**1** **Dates:** Specific dates during which those standards will be taught.

**2** **Instructional Cycle(s):** Based on your school calendar and instructional calendar of assessments, establish an instructional cycle to guide year-long planning. It may be as broad as Semesters or Trimesters, as granular as Weeks 1–36, or somewhere in between with 5–6 week cycles based on interim assessments. Remember, assessments drive your instructional cycle.

**3** **Standards:** Remember this is where we began the journey—defining what students need to know and be able to do. Here in your map you list the specific Anchor Standards and Grade Level Specific Standards that will be covered in each instructional cycle.

**4** **Assessment:** How will you assess mastery of these standards? List any and all assessments that you are aware of at this time. Generally this level of planning looks at summative assessments for these standards. Formative Assessments will be listed with specificity as we go through the levels of instructional design.

**5** **Instructional Materials:** This element of the map is intentionally placed as the last column. Instructional Materials are any and all materials used to teach. At this macro level we want to begin to define instructional materials that will be used for the instructional cycle or to teach this set of standards. Specific, more granular details will be documented deeper in the process. Keep in mind that instructional materials should not drive our planning. Standards, student experiences and student thinking should drive the planning and only then should instructional materials be aligned. Materials are selected based on the standards being taught and the pedagogy being used to teach. The year-long map provides a space to document high-level notes about instructional materials. It is a good place to document what core materials or text that you have available that align to the standards for that cycle. How they will be specifically used and additional materials can be defined later in the process.

**6** **Tasks, Activities, and Experiences:** At a big picture level, establish the experiences, activities and tasks that students will do across the year. Look for gaps and overlaps across the year and across grade levels; these elements are often left off the big picture map. Creating 21st century plans requires the focus to be on the thinking and experiences we create for students. For example, if students write an autobiography in 3rd grade, they should not write one again in 4th or 5th or 8th; this writing project is often seen across grade levels at a single school. Although one could argue the value of this project at various stages of a student's life and in the writing process, we encourage varied and connected options across grade level spans. If a project is being done such as autobiographies at various grade levels, then it should be intentional with clear purpose communicated among teachers. Communicating across grade levels with maps is vital to the design process.

**7** **Cognitive Growth Targets:** This column in the map allows you to look at the big picture through the lens of higher-order thinking. Looking at the tasks, activities, and experiences you have defined for the instructional cycle, begin to list the Cognitive Growth Targets that students will have the opportunity to engage in during that instructional cycle. Ask: does the cycle provide opportunity for creation, metacognition and self-actualization? Keep in mind that the year-long map is the highest level in the design process and therefore is big picture details. We must think about these elements all the way through the process. It allows us to ensure that we have coherent plans and that we don't lose sight of the importance of cognitive growth in all levels of planning.

As we go through the instructional design process, you will find that the same elements often exist or repeat in the different levels of planning. The process becomes more specific and granular as we move through the levels of planning. Remember when building your plan that different levels require different points of view and levels of specificity and detail.

## Building Units of Study: Unit Planning

Unit planning looks at the next level in the instructional design process and focuses on a specific instructional cycle or segment of time. The unit plan builds from the TAA Year-Long Map and provides more detail and specificity for teaching and learning expectations. The unit planning level allows the teacher to consider the connected concepts and thinking that will be taught and experienced over several days up to weeks of time. The unit plan provides teachers a place to document the thinking around big ideas, experiences, activities, pedagogy, and assessments that will be used to meet the student objectives. Keep in mind the lesson plan level will then incorporate this unit overview planning into daily lessons.

When building unit plans, it isn't always about the amount of words on the paper but about the thinking and collaboration each teacher does in planning. The unit plan may not always be completely filled in before teaching. As you build units, teach, and reflect, the units will be added to and refined over time. Unit plans connect the daily learning and big ideas across the weeks and school years.

## Unit Plan Template

**TEACHER AS ARCHITECT: UNIT PLAN**

Dates: ①

Instructional Cycle(s): ②

Themes: ③

Essential Questions: ④

Interdisciplinary Connections: ⑤

Standards: ⑥

Cognitive Growth Targets: ⑦

Learning Objectives: ⑧

Academic Vocabulary: ⑨

Instructional Materials: ⑩

Unit Plan Outline / Thinking Map / White Space: 11

**Student Learning Experiences:**
Describe the Experiences, Activities, and Tasks that students will engage in during this unit:

⑫

Cognitive Growth Targets:

| Student Learning Experiences | Retrieving | Comprehending | Analyzing | Reasoning | Creating | Metacognition | Self-Actualization |
|---|---|---|---|---|---|---|---|
| | | | | | | | |
| | | | | | | | |
| | | | | | | | |
| | | | | | | | |
| | | | | | | | |
| | | | | | | | |
| | | | | | | | |
| | | | | | | | |

**Student Learning Evidence:**
Describe the Assessments in this unit:

⑬

| Check type of Assessment: | | | | | | |
|---|---|---|---|---|---|---|
| | Informal Checks | Observation | Constructed Response | Selected Response | Conference | Performance Assessment |
| | | | | | | |
| | | | | | | |
| | | | | | | |
| | | | | | | |

**Students Monitoring their own Learning?**

⑭

How will students track their progress throughout the unit?

**Pedagogy:**
List Standards and indicate type of pedagogy that will be used to teach that standard in this unit.

**15**

| | Direct | Inquiry | Const-ructivist | Other |
|---|---|---|---|---|
| | | | | |
| | | | | |
| | | | | |
| | | | | |
| | | | | |

**21st Century Skills:**

**16**

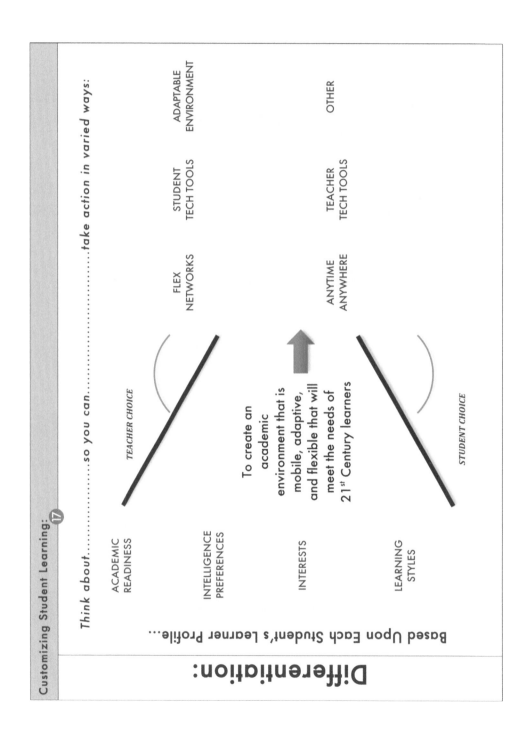

**Customizing Student Learning:** ⑰

*Think about* ...............*so you can* ............*take action in varied ways:*

TEACHER CHOICE

FLEX NETWORKS

STUDENT TECH TOOLS

ADAPTABLE ENVIRONMENT

To create an academic environment that is mobile, adaptive, and flexible that will meet the needs of 21st Century learners

ANYTIME ANYWHERE

TEACHER TECH TOOLS

OTHER

STUDENT CHOICE

ACADEMIC READINESS

INTELLIGENCE PREFERENCES

INTERESTS

LEARNING STYLES

**Based Upon Each Student's Learner Profile...**

**Differentiation:**

## Re-Teaching Unit Standards: 18

| How often will I monitor students' progress throughout the unit?<br><br>What Informal Checks for Understanding will you use to do this? | How will I re-teach content throughout the unit? | What instructional strategies will I use to re-teach content throughout the unit? | What Instructional Materials/Tech Tools will I use for re-teaching content throughout the unit?: | Notes: |
|---|---|---|---|---|
| | | | | |

## Re-Teaching Standards from previous units / benchmark assessments / other:

| What standards from previous units will need to be re-taught during this unit and for which students? | How will I re-teach these standards? | What instructional strategies will I use to re-teach these standards? | What Instructional Materials/Tech Tools will I use for re-teaching these standards? | How will I monitor success of the re-teach: |
|---|---|---|---|---|
| | | | | |

**Parents-As-Partners:** ⑲

Consider:

- Parent friendly unit standards & skills sent home prior to start of unit
- Performance task / other rubrics sent home
- Share Web Links, Text Links
- How parents can support learning:

Other:

**Teacher Notes:** ⑳

**Unit Reflection:** 21

Using the TAA Unit Plan Template:

**1** **Dates:** List the specific dates the unit will be taught.

**2** **Instructional Cycle(s):** Indicate the instructional cycle or cycles in which this unit will take place. Examples: 1st Quarter and/or Cycle 2, and/or Week 4–8. See instructional calendar and your year-long map for information.

**3** **Themes:** Indicate the connecting themes in the unit. Themes can be topic/content oriented or conceptual based.

**4** **Essential Questions:** Set up learning inquiry about the content and concepts within the unit. Essential questions highlight and provoke thought about the big ideas from the standards.

**5** **Interdisciplinary Connections:** Document any opportunities for interdisciplinary connections on content, activities, tasks, readings, materials, etc.

**6** **Standards:** Indicate both anchor and grade-level standards for ELA and practice and content standards for math.

**7** **Cognitive Growth Targets:** Indicate the Cognitive Growth Targets that align to the standards for this unit and will be used to build the teaching and learning of the unit.

**8** **Learning Objectives:** Statements about what a student will be able to do or demonstrate knowledge of, as a result of experiencing the unit. This section can repeat, go more granular on skills, and/or extend on the standards.

**9** **Academic Vocabulary:** Indicate content and conceptual thinking vocabulary that students will need to learn, experience and use for success in the unit.

**10** **Instructional Materials:** Indicate all materials you will use and/or need to find to effectively teach this unit (text, supplemental materials, visuals, digital content, etc.).

⑪ **White Space:** After completing page one of the unit plan, reflect on the learning and thinking that has been identified for the unit. This white space is provided for you to think, draw, and/or map your unit plan and ideas.

⑫ **Student Learning Experiences:** Describe the experiences, activities and tasks that students will engage in during the unit. Determine which CGT these align with and check off the matching box. Use this information to assure that you are planning for higher-order thinking and varied thinking that will span the target. If your choices are not varied across the targets and/or do not reach higher levels of thinking, alter your plan now. Placing all the student experiences in one place early in the unit planning process can be very beneficial to creating a purposeful, balanced, meaningful set of experiences for students aligned to the unit goals.

⑬ **Student Learning Evidence:** Describe the assessments that will take place during the unit. Indicate the type of assessment. Be sure to align the assessments with the previously established elements of the unit plan: standards, Cognitive Growth Targets, academic vocabulary, essential questions, etc.

⑭ **Students Monitoring Their Own Learning:** Indicate the opportunities students will have to track their own progress and learning throughout the unit.

⑮ **Pedagogy:** Based on the standards and Cognitive Growth Targets identified for this unit, determine which pedagogy is best aligned to teach them. Document the unit layout for pedagogy here, aiming for varied learning and alignment. Pedagogy is discussed in detail in Chapter 5: Four Colliding Forces.

⑯ **21st Century Skills:** Document the 21st Century Skills that will be taught and experienced in the unit. Refer to Chapter 6 for 21st Century Skills.

⑰ **Customizing Learning:** Use the following mind map to indicate how you will differentiate in this unit. Chapter 6 outlines the process for customizing and differentiation.

⑱ **Re-Teaching:** Re-teaching occurs throughout the unit of study. Re-teaching needs are determined through all levels of assessment. As you plan your unit, determine ways in which you will monitor learning and plan for re-teaching opportunities. Chapter 10 explores ways to analyze data and plan for student success.

⑲ **Parents as Partners:** Indicate ways in which parents can support student learning. Communicating unit standards and objectives to parents creates a partnership focused on student success.

⑳ **Teacher Notes:** This section is for notes about the unit that are helpful for you as you are teaching the unit and for future reference. This section can be used for content, teaching, or student information and is intended to be customized by the teacher for use.

㉑ **Unit Reflection:** This section is specifically for reflecting on the teaching and learning that occurred during the unit. It should be used throughout and at the conclusion of the unit to record thoughts, questions and actions.

**Here are some questions to guide your unit reflection:**

1. How did students do? Did my assessments provide evidence of student learning? Did my assessments align to the stated objectives? Did my activities and tasks align to what was assessed?

2. Did the activities, experiences, and tasks that my students engaged in yield the cognitive growth I intended? If not, how can I tweak those activities to reach the intended targets? What activities can be re-designed? Which need to be eliminated? Which are the keepers?

3. What were unintended consequences and successes of the plan (if any)?

4. What unit modifications do you recommend?

5. What teacher learnings did you experience during this unit?

## The Daily Lesson

Now it is time to get specific about the learning details! The daily lesson is the most granular way in which teachers describe the step-by-step specific things they will say and do to create the learning experience in their classroom. The bigger pictures of the year-long map and unit plan connect the blueprint together and provide the path that leads to daily teaching. Having a blueprint for the instructional process helps us assure that we are being strategic and intentional from the beginning about what, when and how we teach.

The Unit Plan begins the deeper thinking and planning for learning and the Lesson Plan details with specificity the HOW.

| The Lesson Planning Process: |
|---|
| Know your students |
| Determine the standards |
| Determine learning objectives |
| Determine assessments, tasks and activities |
| Be intentional, crafting the pedagogy, choose appropriately:<br>– Constructivist theory lesson plans<br>– Direct instruction lesson plans<br>– Inquiry-based design lesson plans<br>– Other |
| Select the instructional materials and tools |
| Deliberately place instructional strategies |
| Plan for and align cognitive growth targets and rigor |
| Build in differentiation for learning around 21st century skills |
| Decide and plan for specific use of student questions within your lesson |
| Visualize student responses and potential misconceptions |
| Plan for checks for understanding |
| **Write out** the plan to be specific about what you will do and say |

In our years of observations, we have seen that teachers who plan with specificity consistently show better results. Teacher as Architect templates are designed to provide a structure and process for teacher thinking to approach lesson planning. Plan with the thinking and experiences you want for your students as a priority, then connect and align all of your choices to reach those goals.

## Pedagogical Models

Chapter 5 introduced three pedagogical models: direct instruction, constructivist, and inquiry-based. TAA has provided lesson plan templates addressing these models. This is the deepest level of the instructional process and requires the most detail and specificity. Keep in mind that varied pedagogical models are needed to address the varied thinking we want students to experience. No one pedagogical model is best, and choice of model should be based on content, thinking, engagement, and time. The templates on the following pages are three popular models in which we have embedded Cognitive Growth Targets, 21st Century Skills, and customizing learning.

## Direct Instruction Model

| TEACHER AS ARCHITECT: **DIRECT INSTRUCTION LESSON PLAN** | | | | |
|---|---|---|---|---|
| DATE: | GRADE: | | CONTENT AREA: | |
| STANDARD(S): | | | | |
| OBJECTIVE(S): | | | | |
| COGNITIVE GROWTH TARGETS: | | | | |
| Time | Lesson Plan Elements | Lesson Plan Activities | Instructional Strategies | Questions |
| | Opening/ Activate prior Knowledge | | | |
| | Teacher Modeling | | | |
| | Guided Practice | | | |
| | Independent Practice | | | |
| | Check For Understanding / Assessment | | | |
| | Closing: Summarize key learning | | | |

| Customizing Student Learning: |
|---|
| Flex Networks: |
| Student Tech Tools: |
| Teacher Tech Tools: |
| Adaptable Environment: |

Anytime, Anywhere:

Modifications & Accommodations / Student Notes:

Materials Preparation / Classroom Set Up:

Notes:

Teacher Notes:

Lesson Reflection:

## Constructivist Model

### TEACHER AS ARCHITECT: **CONSTRUCTIVIST LESSON PLAN**

DATE:                          GRADE:              CONTENT AREA:

STANDARD(S):

OBJECTIVE(S):

COGNITIVE GROWTH TARGETS:

| Time | Essential Components of the Lesson | Lesson Plan Activities | Instructional Strategies | Questions |
|------|-----------------------------------|------------------------|--------------------------|-----------|
|      | Engage                            |                        |                          |           |
|      | Explore                           |                        |                          |           |
|      | Explain                           |                        |                          |           |
|      | Elaborate                         |                        |                          |           |
|      | Evaluate                          |                        |                          |           |

Copyright © 2012. Modern Teacher Press. All rights reserved.

| Customizing Student Learning: |
|---|
| Flex Networks: |
| Student Tech Tools: |
| Teacher Tech Tools: |
| Adaptable Environment: |

Anytime, Anywhere:

Modifications & Accommodations / Student Notes:

Materials Preparation / Classroom Set Up:

Notes:

Teacher Notes:

Lesson Reflection:

Inquiry-Based Lesson Plan 1: Science

## TEACHER AS ARCHITECT: **INQUIRY-BASED LESSON PLAN**

| DATE: | GRADE: | CONTENT AREA: Science |
|---|---|---|

**STANDARD(S):**

**OBJECTIVE(S):**

**COGNITIVE GROWTH TARGETS:**

| Time | Essential Components of the Lesson | Lesson Plan Activities | Instructional Strategies | Questions |
|---|---|---|---|---|
| | Introduction | | | |
| | Question | | | |
| | Wonder | | | |
| | Consider & Predict | | | |
| | Develop | | | |
| | Observe & Record | | | |
| | Discover & Communicate | | | |

Copyright © 2012. Modern Teacher Press. All rights reserved.

| Customizing Student Learning: |
| --- |
| Flex Networks: |
| Student Tech Tools: |
| Teacher Tech Tools: |
| Adaptable Environment: |

Anytime, Anywhere:

Modifications & Accommodations / Student Notes:

Materials Preparation / Classroom Set Up:

Notes:

Teacher Notes:

Lesson Reflection:

## Inquiry-Based Lesson Plan 2: Reading And Writing

### TEACHER AS ARCHITECT: **INQUIRY-BASED LESSON PLAN**

| DATE: | GRADE: | CONTENT AREA: Reading & Writing |
|---|---|---|

**STANDARD(S):**

**OBJECTIVE(S):**

**COGNITIVE GROWTH TARGETS:**

| Time | Essential Components of the Lesson | Lesson Plan Activities | Instructional Strategies | Questions |
|---|---|---|---|---|
| | Curiosity | | | |
| | Investigate & Collaborate | | | |
| | Reason & Create | | | |
| | Communicate | | | |

Copyright © 2012. Modern Teacher Press. All rights reserved.

| Customizing Student Learning: |
| --- |
| Flex Networks: |
| Student Tech Tools: |
| Teacher Tech Tools: |
| Adaptable Environment: |

Anytime, Anywhere:

Modifications & Accommodations / Student Notes:

Materials Preparation / Classroom Set Up:

Notes:

Teacher Notes:

Lesson Reflection:

## The Components of Instructional Design

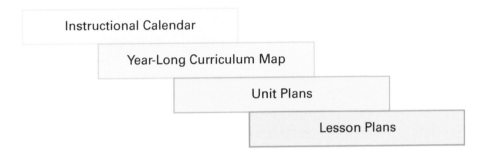

Instructional Calendar

Year-Long Curriculum Map

Unit Plans

Lesson Plans

Trends in planning are showing a variety of uses and cross over with year-long, unit, and lesson planning. The templates and tools provided in this book are intended to guide and focus the planning and teaching process. Keep in mind it is essential to understand the expectations of your district and school for planning and documentation. The templates provided here set up the thinking process to support effective teaching. They reflect the actions we have seen time and time again that our most effective teachers do and are grounded in creating 21st century learning for our students. These templates and habits of mind can be incorporated into any process for planning instruction. You can find these templates stored in our online Digital Resource Library at *teacherasarchitect.com.*

## Putting It All Together—The Alignment Tool

The Alignment Tool is designed as an additional template to guide the design and delivery process throughout planning, teaching, and in reflection. It can be used in many ways to evaluate alignment both during planning and after teaching. The Alignment Tool provides a lens through the Cognitive Growth Targets to analyze elements of the instructional blueprint. The Alignment Tool can be used to analyze an individual lesson, a day of instruction, a week of instruction, or a unit of study within a single classroom. It provides a way for teachers to answer the following kinds of questions:

Over the course of the day, week, lesson, or unit, what opportunities have I provided for my students to…

1) …experience all levels of thinking through the standards?

2) …communicate or demonstrate their learning and understanding?

3) …build learning in different ways?

4) …respond to rigorous questions?

5) …engage in creativity and innovation?

6) …experience and build 21st Century Skills?

7) …to communicate and connect in various formats?

# INSTRUCTIONAL ALIGNMENT TOOL™

| Cognitive Growth Targets | Standard/ Objective | Assessment(s) | Pedagogy | Questions | Tasks/Activities | 21st Century Skills Integration |
|---|---|---|---|---|---|---|
| **Retrieving:** The process of recalling and/ or recognizing declarative, procedural, or conceptual knowledge from memory. | | | | | | |
| **Comprehending:** The process of initial understanding of declarative, procedural, or conceptual knowledge. | | | | | | |
| **Analyzing:** The process of examining knowledge by breaking it down into its components to determine relationships, structures, and/or purpose. | | | | | | |
| **Reasoning:** The process of drawing conclusions and/or making judgments based upon evidence, facts, or criteria. | | | | | | |
| **Creating:** The process of making, inventing, or producing something new. | | | | | | |
| **Metacognition:** The process of being aware of one's own thinking and learning. | | | | | | |
| **Self-actualization:** The process of understanding one's self. | | | | | | |

The Alignment Tool pushes us to think about six specific elements: Objectives/Standards, Assessment, Questions, Pedagogy, Tasks and Activities, 21st Century Skills Integration that occur across our planning and teaching and that need to interact seamlessly to meet the learning goals of our students. The tool supports our methodology for both alignment and rigor.

We have found in our classroom observations across America that too often the established objectives, activities taking place, and how they are being assessed just don't align. Although each element usually seems to be well intended, they are nevertheless not very effective. These six components must be carefully planned for and aligned if we expect to meet the established learning outcomes.

*Teachers have so many components to the teaching process to think about, plan for and then execute that we find it is essential to have a framework and systematic way to approach it all. These tools are designed to connect the parts, provide a design framework and focus on thinking and learning. The Alignment Tool is one way in which to reflect upon rigor in the classroom through an organized lens of Cognitive Growth and 21st century thinking.*

## Blueprint Essentials

The collaboration behind mapping is a key element to effective teaching—planning for instruction across grades eliminates duplication and sets up a progression of learning.

The use of a common professional language and templates for planning and teaching can create a community of information and goals and fosters the opportunity for ongoing dialogue and creation.

Collaborative planning is about the teacher thinking and the dialogue between colleagues that leads to personal growth and learning.

Intentional choices and detailed planning is essential for effective instruction to occur regularly and to meet the levels of rigor needed in the 21st century.

Pedagogy refers to the teacher actions and the order in which they are done to build the learning. Understanding the uses of pedagogy and their alignment to standards and thinking goals is essential.

Students should have the opportunity to experience varied pedagogy within all content areas.

Instructional design is a multi-step and multi-faceted process of inter-related parts. Understanding these relationships and building plans that align all the parts is essential for success.

## Reflection and Action

▶ How do you currently plan for daily instruction?

▶ How do you integrate the multiple components of instructional design?

▶ Take time to think about your current practices...how intentional are your instructional choices?

▶ What is most important to you in the planning process?

▶ How can you take elements of this chapter and use them to strengthen your current practices?

# In the Library

### Curriculum Mapping

*Mapping the Big Picture: Integrating Curriculum and Assessment, K–12 (1997)*
Heidi Hayes Jacobs

*Curriculum 21: Essential Education for a Changing World (2010)*
Heidi Hayes Jacobs

*The Curriculum Mapping Planner: Templates, Tools and Resources for Effective Professional Development, (2004)*
Heidi Hayes Jacobs

*A Guide to Curriculum Mapping: Planning, Implementing, and Sustaining the Process* (2009)
Janet Hale

*Keys to curriculum mapping: Strategies and tools to make it work* (2005)
Susan Udelhofen

http://www.curriculummapping101.com

http://www.curriculum21.com

### Unit Planning

*Understanding by Design* (2005 Expanded 2nd edition)
Grant Wiggins and Jay McTighe

*The Understanding by Design Guide to Creating High Quality Units* (2011)
Grant Wiggins and Jay McTighe

### Lesson Planning and Student Thinking

*The Lesson Plan Handbook: Essential Strategies that Inspire Student Thinking and Learning* (2010)
Peter Brunn

# Journal Entry

**Experiencing and Personalizing your Journey**

At this point in the journey you might be feeling overwhelmed — a natural feeling given the amount of things you need to consider when designing instruction. (Sometimes we think the general public has no idea what goes into being a teacher.) The key at this point is to remember that this is a journey and not a destination. No one is expecting you to have all of the parts of the blueprint your first time through.

Teacher Architect Date: Everyone has a special place to get away from it all. Where is that place for you? Maybe taking a long walk or a hike, the movies, or hanging out in a coffee shop. Make a date with yourself this week. When you do, try to clear your head from all of the noise in education. Begin to think about one or two things you can do to improve your classroom blueprint. Think back to Chapters 1–7. What resonated with you? If you focused on one or two things that could make the biggest difference for your students, what would they be? Then take action.

During this journey, it is important to take care of yourself. We call these "teacher architect dates." We all need to take the time to reflect on our work, find meaning in it, and enjoy the process.

# High-Impact
## Teaching Behaviors

Teach the blueprint by using a series of high-impact behaviors directly associated with student learning.

As we build upon Core Principles 1 and 2, the designing and customizing phase of our classroom blueprint, we introduce Core Principle 3, High-Impact Teaching Behaviors. A highly-effective teacher teaches their instructional blueprint by deliberately using a series of high-impact behaviors demonstrated to improve student learning. We continue our discussion with these questions:

1. What teaching behaviors correlate to student achievement?

2. What do they look like in classroom practice?

Chapter 9—Delivering on the Design examines what these behaviors can accomplish—and what they look like—in real classrooms.

## Core Principle 1
### Designing with Purpose

Design a blueprint for classroom instruction and strategically consider a range of choices to motivate student success.

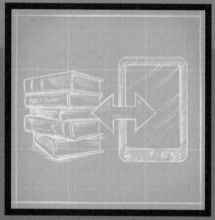

## Core Principle 2
### Customizing 21st Century Learning

Know the 21st century learner, leverage a range of advanced technology tools that will provide multiple learning pathways that customize and enrich the learning experience.

## Core Principle 3
### High-Impact Teaching Behaviors

Teach the blueprint by using a series of high-impact behaviors associated with student learning.

## Core Principle 4
### Managing Student Performance

From multiple sources, collect and analyze evidence of student learning to understand each student's mastery of specific content and readiness for new content.

# High-Impact Teaching Behaviors

Know your 21st Century Learner

Digital Learning Systems

21st Century Tools

Learning Pathways

Learning Environment

Classroom Culture

Instructional Delivery

Student Engagement

Learning Facilitation

Application of Cognitive Growth Targets

© Modern Teacher Press 2012

# Chapter 9

# Delivering
## on the
## Design

# A Teacher's Story: Connecting with the Class

*At an Arizona middle school, Sylvia stood at the door as her fourth period class entered her classroom. "Hi, Johnny. Hello, Tameka. Good morning, Jessie." Sylvia greeted every student as they entered her classroom as she did every day of the school year. Fourth period was difficult—it was right before lunch and seventh graders had the last lunch period of the day, at 12:35.*

*Yet as the bell rang, 33 seventh graders immediately began one of three different warm ups on the white board.*

*Sylvia circulated the room, checking in with each student. Four minutes into the period, Sylvia had greeted everybody, checked in with each student about the previous night's homework, taken attendance, and differentiated a warm up exercise for 33 students. During her prep period earlier in the day, Sylvia logged onto her school's digital learning system and monitored which students were able to access her re-teach playlist from the day before via their home access account. She would use this data to differentiate her morning warm up. She then projected a digital image onto her interactive white board and posed a question to the class: What judgment would you make about the man in this image? What information did you use to make that conclusion?*

## Connect and Reflect

At this point in our journey through *Teacher as Architect*, you have begun a plan for designing effective instruction that is complex and has many shifting components.

But what happens when all of the planning is finished? When the first child walks into that classroom—the space you designed, both for content and for space? Because it is at that moment that *teaching begins*. And the research is pretty clear that **what we do as educators does matter in the lives of students: in both what we say to students and what we do *not* say to students.** It makes a difference to students in how we discipline and praise them. How we ask questions. What we expect. All of these things matter— and they matter in an important way.

It may seem obvious, maybe even intuitive, that what a teacher says or does plays a critical role in how a student learns. However, for many years in our profession, people have chalked that up to an *art*. We've heard many times good teaching explained as a gift people are born with. Yet while there is an artfulness to it, there is *science* behind it. **We don't just believe in good teachers—we believe in good teaching. Highly-effective teaching can be taught**. Highly-effective teaching is the sum of all the little details that are all correlated to behaviors. As our journey unfolds we are asked to think about teaching behaviors. What behaviors did Sylvia use that you would consider effective?

## Why We Do What We Do

While research over the past several decades has focused on a few grain-size behaviors and their impact on student learning, some in the profession are beginning to tie the studies together and develop useful tools for practitioners. These game changers call for the creation of a common language—and purposeful coaching tools.

### How Do We Talk About Effective Teaching?

Marzano explains that, "All teachers and administrators in a district or school building should be able to describe effective teaching in a similar way." To aid in this goal, he built a taxonomy of 41 effective practices and categorized them into three groups: **Routine Strategies, Content Strategies, and On-the-Spot Strategies**. Similarly, Joseph Wise and David Sundstrom conducted a meta-analysis of teaching behaviors linked to increasing students' academic performance. In their highly-successful (and recommended) book, *The Power of Teaching*, they built a coaching tool around 44 effective teaching behaviors and categorized them into six power sources.

| 1.0 | Cognitive Connections for Learning (and Teaching) |
|-----|-----|
| 2.0 | Pacing and Productivity for Learning |
| 3.0 | Transitions, Processes and Endings for Learning |
| 4.0 | On-Task Learning |
| 5.0 | Differentiated Teaching to Accelerate Learning |
| 6.0 | Aligned Expectations to Macro Organization |

In addition to Marzano's work and the work of Wise and Sundstrom, Deborah Loewenberg Ball and Francesca Forzani, in the December 2010/January 2011 issue of *Educational Leadership*, wrote an article titled "Teaching Skillful Teaching," in which they set out to identify high-leverage teaching practices. Their research focused in on two specific behaviors associated with teaching effectiveness: **making expertise explicit and seeing the world through students' eyes**.

To make expertise explicit, the authors suggest that the teacher needs to "unpack" academic content and concepts and make them accessible to and learnable by students. This requires the teacher to foster two distinct skill sets—the first, knowing the content and second, the ability to break the content and concepts down into small chunks for the learner (from the learner's perspective) and then put it back together again.

To effectively do the second requires executing a host of behaviors at every step of the lesson. Granular behaviors like launching a lesson, giving feedback to students, checking for student understanding, questioning students, managing behavior, tying up discussions, and crafting norms for student-to-student interactions were all studied in Ball and Forzani's research. Some of the behaviors appear on our list below.

For a teacher to see the world through students' eyes the authors suggest that teachers need to teach their lessons from the perspective of their learners. Just because the teacher learned how to multiply fractions a particular way or write a five-paragraph essay using a specific approach does not mean every student will be successful in a similar way. Teachers need to develop **sophisticated learner profiles** (as described in chapter 6) of their students and be constantly on the lookout for how students perceive the lesson. Seeing the world through your students' eyes translates into actionable teaching behaviors when executing your instructional blueprint.

**The Growth Mindset** is the fundamental belief that all kids can learn or intelligence is changeable, whereas the fixed mindset believes intelligence is determined at birth and cannot be changed. Dweck and Molden (2005) challenged the fixed mindset assumptions in their work on motivation and self-theories. Dweck (2006) further addresses the role motivation can play in *Mindset* and provides a rich supply of evidence that teacher and student belief systems matter when it comes to teacher-to-student interactions and student achievement. Teachers play a critical role in helping students see value in a growth mindset, both in how they perceive students' academic capacities as well as how they teach their students to see their own academic potential.

## Guiding Questions

▶ Why do you think it is important for teachers to reflect on the teaching behaviors they use in classroom instruction?

▶ Why do some behaviors correlate to student success and others do not?

▶ How do you get feedback on your teaching behaviors?

▶ What conditions make feedback helpful? What conditions make feedback *not* helpful?

# Connecting to Classroom Practice

In this chapter, we explore the *behavioral sciences* of teaching. We assert that *how* a teacher behaves with students—both their actions *and* reactions while they are teaching—matter. The research is clear that there are some teaching behaviors that have a positive correlation (causal relationship) with student achievement. We call these High-Impact Teaching (HIT) behaviors.

## High-Impact Teaching Behaviors (HIT)

Wise and Sundstrom's research discovered 44 teaching behaviors that have a profound impact on student achievement. We have found their research extremely helpful in our work with teachers. This chapter, in part, builds upon that work and is meant to help teachers think about how the design of their blueprint is effectively executed.

There are two underlying reasons we build upon the work of Wise and Sundstrom and offer an updated tool.

1. We have simplified the behaviors from 44 to 25. This shorter list helps teachers focus on a smaller set of high-impact behaviors. (Our own meta-analysis includes some new behaviors from more recent publications and research.)

2. Our HIT 25 list is hierarchical. This will help focus coaching sessions. There are some behaviors teachers need to first have a solid grasp of before attending to others.

Our own meta-analysis of teaching behaviors that affect student learning introduce "grain size" behaviors that are meant to be broken down into discrete and isolated actions. We then organize the behaviors into a hierarchical model to be used as a coaching tool to further develop and strengthen teaching practices. When teaching behaviors in a classroom "HIT" the target, the likelihood that student learning increases improves as well.

| | Pedagogy | Instructional Strategies | High-Impact Teaching Behaviors |
|---|---|---|---|
| **Definition** | Pedagogy is the way in which you build learning within a lesson: the order of and the specific steps or elements of the lesson that will be used to build/scaffold/create the learning experience for students. | Instructional choices that support the pedagogy, thinking, and learning goals selected for the lesson. Instructional strategies assist in setting up the learning experience students will go through during the lesson. | Specific teaching behaviors that have a positive correlation (causal relationship) with student achievement. |
| **Example** | Constructivist | Open-ended/probing questioning<br><br>Think-Pair-Share | Sufficient wait time<br><br>Effectively guiding incorrect answers |

## HIT the Target

To fully execute on your instructional blueprint you will first want to think about the physical learning environment you will create for students. Then, imagine your students entering this environment. How do you want them to behave? What routines will you teach them? What will be displayed on the walls? All the little details matter in a big way. Take the time to plan—and then teach your students.

The 25 behaviors listed below are organized for complexity. As the behavioral lists progresses, the teaching behaviors become more nuanced.

# HIT 25 LIST

## A Ready-to-Learn Environment

1. Strategic Arrangement of Furniture

2. Behavior Management System in Place

3. Pre-Established Routines and Procedures

4. Teacher Artifacts, Graphic Organizers and Academic Anchors

5. Student Work Displayed

## Classroom Culture: Directing Student Behavior

6. Positive Framing—The Strategic Use of Positive Reinforcement

7. Redirect Inappropriate Behavior/Strategically Stop Misconduct

## Classroom Culture and Learning Facilitation:
## Crafting an Academically Caring Classroom, Pacing, and Building Relationships

8. Growth Mindset: Demonstrating High Expectations for Low Expectancy Students

9. Bell-to-Bell Instruction

10. Maintain Academic Flow and Pacing

11. Circulate and assist with Instructional Purpose

12. Questioning with Sufficient Wait Time

13. Seeing the World Through Your Students' Eyes

14. Effectively Guiding Incorrect Answers by Probing to Understand Student Misconceptions

15. Applied Specific Academic Praise

16. Check for Academic Understanding

## Student Engagement

**17.** Specific Dialogue to Excite Learning

**18.** Managing Student Response Rates

**19.** Student-to-Student Academic Talk

## Application of Rigor Through Cognitive Growth Targets

**20.** Strategic Use of Analysis, Reasoning, Creating Questions and Tasks

**21.** Strategic Use of Metacognition and Self-Actualization Questions and Tasks

**22.** Application of Real-World Relevance and Primary Sources

## Application and Instructional Delivery of Customized Teaching

**23.** Strategic Use of Technology to Increase the Instructional Impact

▶ Appropriate use of technology to: manage flexible networks; facilitate anywhere, anytime learning; and leverage digital content

**24.** Differentiation to Facilitate Learning

▶ Based upon 21st century learners and their learner profiles

**25.** Embedded Application of 21st Century Skills

**TASK:** Study our HIT 25 List. The templates in the following pages are provided as a reflection tool for your use. Read through our examples of what it looks like in classroom practice. For the next few months, select one or two behaviors each week. After teaching a lesson, or at the end of the school day, write down some of your thoughts on the specific behavior you were focusing on. What did you notice? What resonated? Which behaviors were easy for you? Which were more challenging?

# HIT Reflection Tools

| HIT 25<br>1 of 25 | Strategic Arrangement of Furniture |
|---|---|

| What it looks like in classroom practice | |
|---|---|
| **Low-Impact Behaviors** | **High-Impact Behaviors** |
| • Student desks are arranged with little flexibility to rearrange furniture for in-the-moment lessons<br>• Student desks and ancillary furniture are arranged in such a way that makes it difficult to move around the room<br>• Teacher desk is positioned as the center of learning, symbolically representing that the flow of knowledge must pass through the teacher | • Student desks are adaptable, flexible, and arranged with purpose<br>• Student desks and ancillary furniture are arranged to make it easy to move around the room<br>• Teacher desk is positioned as a secondary factor, leveraging the arrangement of student desks first to facilitate learning |

**Reflection on the delivery:**

| HIT 25 2 of 25 | Behavior Management System in Place |
|---|---|

| What it looks like in classroom practice | |
|---|---|
| **Low-Impact Behaviors** | **High-Impact Behaviors** |
| • Lack of clearly defined rules and expectations for behavior<br><br>• Inconsistent, vague, or unknown expectations for classroom activities and transitions<br><br>• Inconsistent feedback from teacher about behavioral expectations<br><br>• Little or no time has been given to teaching behavioral expectations<br><br>• Little or no time has been given to revisiting or re-teaching behavioral expectations throughout the school year | • Clearly defined rules and expectations for behavior are present<br><br>• Explicit expectations for all classroom activities and transitions<br><br>• Consistent feedback regarding behavior is present<br><br>• Time has been devoted to teaching the behavior management system to students<br><br>• Time is scheduled to revisit and re-teach behavioral expectations throughout the school year |

**Reflection on the delivery:**

| HIT 25<br>3 of 25 | Pre-Established Routines and Procedures |
| --- | --- |

| What it looks like in classroom practice ||
| --- | --- |
| **Low-Impact Behaviors** | **High-Impact Behaviors** |
| • Lack of clearly-defined routines and procedures for classroom management | • Clearly-defined routines and procedures for classroom management are present, including: transitions, materials, clerical tasks, student needs (restroom breaks, meals, water, etc) |

**Reflection on the delivery:**

| HIT 25 4 of 25 | Teacher Artifacts, Graphic Organizers and Academic Anchors |
| --- | --- |

| What it looks like in classroom practice | |
| --- | --- |
| **Low-Impact Behaviors** | **High-Impact Behaviors** |
| • Teacher artifacts, graphic organizers, and academic anchors **do not** reflect the current content being taught | • Teacher artifacts, graphic organizers, and academic anchors reflect the current content being taught |
| • Store-bought artifacts cover wall space but are not academically relevant to the content | • Store-bought artifacts are used strategically to scaffold and build learning |
| • Teacher artifacts and academic anchors are not timely, are dated, and are not used strategically during teaching | • Teacher artifacts and academic anchors are timely, rotate with new content, and are used strategically during teaching |
| • A one-size-fits-all approach is used with graphic organizers and is often selected by the teacher | • Graphic organizers represent a range of options for organizing information and students are given choice in selecting or creating how they will organize the content they are learning |

**Reflection on the delivery:**

| HIT 25 5 of 25 | Student Work Displayed |
|---|---|

| What it looks like in classroom practice ||
|---|---|
| **Low-Impact Behaviors** | **High-Impact Behaviors** |
| • There is a lack of student work displayed in the classroom<br>• Student work displayed in the classroom is outdated with little meaning to the current content being studied | • The teacher has created a print-rich learning environment for students using student-generated work |

**Reflection on the delivery:**

| HIT 25 6 of 25 | Positive Framing Strategic Use of Positive Reinforcement |
|---|---|

| What it looks like in classroom practice ||
|---|---|
| **Low-Impact Behaviors** | **High-Impact Behaviors** |
| • Loss-framed messages<br>• Using sarcasm and embarrassment<br>• Motivation through negative consequences | • Teacher establishes a positive academic environment by praising students often<br>• All interactions begin with positive assumptions or message<br>• Systemic recognition of positive behavior and academic accomplishments<br>• Evidence of compassion |

**Reflection on the delivery:**

| HIT 25 7 of 25 | Redirect Inappropriate Behavior and Strategically Stop Misconduct |
|---|---|

| What it looks like in classroom practice | |
|---|---|
| **Low-Impact Behaviors** | **High-Impact Behaviors** |
| • Over-reliance on negative consequences and punitive discipline<br>• Applying discipline without understanding of behavior<br>• Non-systemic delivery of intervention techniques<br>• Becoming emotional when addressing undesirable behavior<br>• Escalating situations through voice volume and actions | • Systemic progression of intervention techniques<br>• Remaining calm and resolute<br>• Only when necessary, clear and consistent application of negative consequences |

**Reflection on the delivery:**

Classroom Culture: Directing Student Behavior

| HIT 25<br>8 of 25 | Growth Mindset: Demonstrating High Expectations<br>for Low-Expectancy Students |
|---|---|

| What it looks like in classroom practice | |
|---|---|
| **Low-Impact Behaviors** | **High-Impact Behaviors** |
| • Focusing on what a student cannot do<br><br>• Using challenging circumstances as an excuse for low expectations<br><br>• Treating IEP's as a compliance document | • Praising effort and hard work<br><br>• Setting SMART goals with individual students and groups of students<br><br>• Focusing on how a student can be supported<br><br>• Having an internal locus of control to influence student outcomes<br><br>• Utilizing IEP's as a continuous and ongoing plan for student improvement |

**Reflection on the delivery:**

| HIT 25
9 of 25 | Bell-to-Bell Instruction |
|---|---|

| What it looks like in classroom practice | |
|---|---|
| **Low-Impact Behaviors** | **High-Impact Behaviors** |
| • Lesson beginning is slow and unclear<br>• Time is wasted because of confusion and lack of lesson clarity<br>• Materials are not pre-sorted<br>• Lesson ends with too much instructional time left | • Immediate and focused start to instruction<br>• Explicit directions and check for clarity<br>• Circulates room to monitor expectations<br>• Materials are pre-sorted and ready to go<br>• Every minute of instructional time is used strategically |

**Reflection on the delivery:**

*Classroom Culture and Learning Facilitation*

| HIT 25<br>10 of 25 | Maintained Academic Flow and Pacing |
|---|---|

| What it looks like in classroom practice ||
|---|---|
| **Low-Impact Behaviors** | **High-Impact Behaviors** |
| • Multi-step directions are given all at once, leaving students confused<br><br>• Multi-step directions are only stated verbally, leaving some students confused<br><br>• Teacher talks over students as they transition without full direction<br><br>• Expectations are unclear and inconsistent | • Directions are clear, broken down into manageable chunks, and articulated in concise language<br><br>• Directions are both verbal and written<br><br>• Teacher uses a range of strategies to transition students from task to task<br><br>• Teacher checks for understanding of directions before transitions happen<br><br>• Expectations are clear and consistent |

**Reflection on the delivery:**

| HIT 25 11 of 25 | Circulate and Assist with Instructional Purpose |
| --- | --- |

| What it looks like in classroom practice | |
| --- | --- |
| **Low-Impact Behaviors** | **High-Impact Behaviors** |
| • Sitting at desk<br>• Wandering around room without purpose<br>• Focused attention on a few students | • Circulate the classroom, check all students for engagement<br>• Strategic feedback and coaching<br>• Check for understanding for all students |

**Reflection on the delivery:**

Classroom Culture and Learning Facilitation

**HIT 25**
**12 of 25**

**Questioning with Sufficient Wait Time**

| What it looks like in classroom practice | |
|---|---|
| **Low-Impact Behaviors** | **High-Impact Behaviors** |
| • Designing questions "on the fly"<br>• Not enough wait time<br>• Too much wait time<br>• Random calling out | • Designing questions in advance<br>• Strategic use of wait time<br>• Strategic use of probing questions<br>• Eye contact with students<br>• Appropriate use of think time |

**Reflection on the delivery:**

| HIT 25<br>13 of 25 | Seeing the World Through Students' Eyes |
|---|---|

| What it looks like in classroom practice | |
|---|---|
| **Low-Impact Behaviors** | **High-Impact Behaviors** |
| • Teacher teaches content the way they learned it, leaving no other option for students to access content<br>• Content is delivered without any scaffolding, leaving students to break down the content on their own<br>• Lesson is taught mostly whole group | • Teacher considers the types of misconceptions students may have with the content and provides multiple approaches for students to access the content<br>• Teacher unpacks the content by breaking concepts into small chunks and then puts it back together again<br>• Teacher uses both whole-to-part and part-to-whole approach when teaching content<br>• Teacher considers the range of learner profiles within the classroom and provides multiple opportunities for diverse learners to access the content |

**Reflection on the delivery:**

*Classroom Culture and Learning Facilitation*

| HIT 25 14 of 25 | Effectively Guiding Incorrect Answers by Probing to Understand Student Misconceptions |
|---|---|

| What it looks like in classroom practice ||
|---|---|
| **Low-Impact Behaviors** | **High-Impact Behaviors** |
| • Teacher moves on without understanding who has "got it" <br> • Teacher avoids calling on students perceived to not know the answer <br> • Teacher dismisses student response by quickly searching for a student with the correct answer <br> • No feedback is given when an incorrect answer is given | • Teacher uses incorrect answers as a "teaching moment" <br> • High rates of, and strategic use of, probing questions to understand student misconceptions <br><br> *Examples include:* <br> • Can you be more specific? <br> • Can you give me an example of what you are thinking? <br> • Can you restate or say what ____ said in your own words? <br> • Does anyone have the same answer but a different way to say it? <br> • Does anyone have a different answer or thought? <br> • Can you tell me a little more? |

**Reflection on the delivery:**

| HIT 25<br>15 of 25 | Applied Specific Academic Praise |
|---|---|

| What it looks like in classroom practice ||
|---|---|
| **Low-Impact Behaviors** | **High-Impact Behaviors** |
| • General praise like "good job" | • Specific praise connected to academic content, "Jennifer, I liked the way you remembered to drop the y before adding ing" |

**Reflection on the delivery:**

Classroom Culture and Learning Facilitation

Classroom Culture and Learning Facilitation

| HIT 25 16 of 25 | Check for Academic Understanding |
|---|---|

| What it looks like in classroom practice ||
|---|---|
| **Low-Impact Behaviors** | **High-Impact Behaviors** |
| • Generally questions the class, "Does everyone get it?"<br>• Lacks a clear monitoring and recordkeeping system<br>• No indication of pre-planned informal assessments | • Use of individual white boards or other tools to check for individual understanding<br>• Systemic data collection and monitoring system in place<br>• Strategic, pre-planned informal assessments<br>• Multiple opportunities to check for understanding with multi-modal informal assessments |

**Reflection on the delivery:**

| HIT 25<br>17 of 25 | Specific Dialogue to Excite Learning |
|---|---|

| What it looks like in classroom practice | |
|---|---|
| **Low-Impact Behaviors** | **High-Impact Behaviors** |
| • Lecture-style teaching<br>• Teacher does most of the talking and thinking<br>• Focus on a small number of students<br>• Monotone<br>• Low levels of enthusiasm for content and lesson<br>• Apparent lack of interest | • Students do most of the talking and thinking<br>• Engages all students<br>• Varied voice tones<br>• Appropriate levels of enthusiasm for content and lesson<br>• Appropriate level of interest |

**Reflection on the delivery:**

Student Engagement

| HIT 25 18 of 25 | Managing Student Response Rates |
|---|---|

## What it looks like in classroom practice

| Low-Impact Behaviors | High-Impact Behaviors |
|---|---|
| • Calls on a few students during the lesson<br>• Lacks methods and strategies for all students to respond during the lesson<br>• Resists technology to manage student responses | • Engages all students in the lesson<br>• Has several methods and strategies for all students to respond during the lesson<br>• Leverages technology to manage student responses<br>• Facilitates student responses outside the classroom |

**Reflection on the delivery:**

| HIT 25 19 of 25 | Student-to-Student Academic Talk |
| --- | --- |

**Student Engagement**

| What it looks like in classroom practice | |
| --- | --- |
| **Low-Impact Behaviors** | **High-Impact Behaviors** |
| • Students interact with academic content only through the teacher<br>• Low rates of academic talk with each other<br>• There is a consistent pattern of student-to-teacher-to-student dialogue | • Students are given multiple opportunities to talk about academic content with their peers<br>• High rates of turn and talk facilitate student engagement<br>• There is a consistent pattern of student-to-teacher-to-student dialogue *before* the teacher interjects their own thinking |

**Reflection on the delivery:**

| HIT 25 20 of 25 | Strategic Use of Analysis, Reasoning, Creating Questions and Tasks |
|---|---|

| What it looks like in classroom practice | |
|---|---|
| **Low-Impact Behaviors** | **High-Impact Behaviors** |
| High rates of the following types of questions:<br><br>• Label_____.<br>• Identify the____.<br>• Define each term.<br>• List the _____.<br>• Illustrate_____.<br>• When did_____ take place?<br>• What happened first?<br>• Do you recognize_____? | High rates of the following types of questions:<br><br>• Is this the most effective approach____?<br>• Prioritize the steps to solve this problem.<br>• Classify ____ according to_____.<br>• What is the pattern_____?<br>• What caused _____ to happen?<br>• Propose a solution for_____.<br>• What changes to_____ would you recommend?<br>• How would you interpret____?<br>• Can you justify_____?<br>• How would you critique_____?<br>• Why did you select that_____?<br>• What arguments/evidence was more convincing?<br>• Is this the most effective approach?<br>• Build_____.<br>• Invent____.<br>• Create____. |

**Reflection on the delivery:**

| HIT 25<br>21 of 25 | Strategic Use of Metacognition and<br>Self-Actualization Questions and Tasks |
|---|---|

| What it looks like in classroom practice | |
|---|---|
| **Low-Impact Behaviors** | **High-Impact Behaviors** |
| High rates of the following types of questions:<br><br>• Find_____.<br>• List the steps you used to_____.<br>• Estimate the following_____.<br>• What information is missing?<br>• What is the main idea?<br>• Which one_____. | High rates of the following types of questions:<br><br>• Explain your thinking on that.<br>• Can you tell me how you came to that conclusion?<br>• What strategy or thinking did you use to solve that?<br>• What are you left thinking/wondering about?<br>• What do you do when things don't go well?<br>• When are you most happy?<br>• How do you feel when___?<br>• Why do you believe that?<br>• What motivates you?<br>• How are you part of your community? |

**Reflection on the delivery:**

*Application of Rigor through Cognitive Growth Targets*

## Application of Real-World Relevance and Primary Sources

| What it looks like in classroom practice | |
|---|---|
| **Low-Impact Behaviors** | **High-Impact Behaviors** |
| • Little or no primary sources are used during lessons<br>• Student work is worksheet-based<br>• Student work is primarily textbook-driven<br>• Tasks and assignments lack real-world application and are seen as compliance exercises | • Primary sources like newspapers, historical documents, websites, blogs, artifacts, etc...are used in lessons<br>• Student work is authentic<br>• Student work extends well beyond the textbook<br>• Tasks and assignments often involved real-world context, simulations, and have purpose and meaning for students |

**Reflection on the delivery:**

| HIT 25 23 of 25 | Strategic Use of Technology to Increase the Instructional Impact |
|---|---|

| What it looks like in classroom practice | |
|---|---|
| **Low-Impact Behaviors** | **High-Impact Behaviors** |
| • Technology is the primary point of the lesson<br><br>• High usage of digital media is used whole class as the primary teaching strategy | • Technology is leveraged as a tool to customize and personalize instruction<br><br>• Digital media is leveraged to differentiate the instructional process and product<br><br>• Students use the technology to create content |

**Reflection on the delivery:**

Application and Instructional Delivery of Customized Teaching

| HIT 25<br>24 of 25 | **Application of Real-World Relevance and Primary Sources** |
|---|---|

| **What it looks like in classroom practice** | |
|---|---|
| **Low-Impact Behaviors** | **High-Impact Behaviors** |
| • Little to no evidence that the teacher considers the diversity of learners within the classroom<br>• Instruction is often whole group and targeted to the "middle" | • Clear evidence that instruction is personalized and customized based upon several factors in each student's learner profile |

**Reflection on the delivery:**

| HIT 25<br>25 of 25 | Embedded Application of 21st Century Skills |
| --- | --- |

| What it looks like in classroom practice | |
| --- | --- |
| **Low-Impact Behaviors** | **High-Impact Behaviors** |
| • Lessons are low level and the teacher does most of the thinking<br><br>• Students rarely talk to each other about their work<br><br>• Little evidence of information and digital media literacy present in lessons<br><br>• Lessons are all teacher-directed with little choice for students | • Lessons involve critical thinking and problem-solving skills<br><br>• Students communicate and collaborate about their work<br><br>• Teacher utilizes and requires student proficiency with information literacy and digital media literacy<br><br>• Teacher provides opportunities for students to take their own academic initiative and direction, provides leadership opportunities, and adapts the process within each unit<br><br>• Students are creators of digital content |

**Reflection on the delivery:**

Application and Instructional Delivery of Customized Teaching

## Application of High-Impact Teaching Behaviors

Once you become familiar with each behavior on the list and are conscious of what it looks like in classroom practice, you may want to consider videotaping yourself in action. Yes, this can be a very intimidating experience—however, it can also be a powerful tool to improve your teaching. Any type of camera will do. Consider filming one lesson. Place it in the back of the classroom, out of the way of your students. It may take you a few times to get the perfect placement to capture the entire room and make sure the audio is clear. When the lesson is complete, download the digital content onto your computer.

Watch the film by focusing in on one specific behavior. Use the templates to document your teaching behaviors. What did you notice? What were some of your high-impact behaviors? Which teaching behaviors could be adjusted from low-impact to high-impact? Remember, this is a journey, not a destination. Applaud yourself for taking a risk. This kind of self-assessment is not an easy thing to do!

## Blueprint Essentials

Teaching behaviors have been correlated to student achievement.

Understanding what teaching behaviors correlate to student success can greatly impact learning for students.

Being aware of unintended consequences based on teaching behaviors is valuable knowledge.

Being aware of, and reflective of, our own teaching behaviors is important to student success.

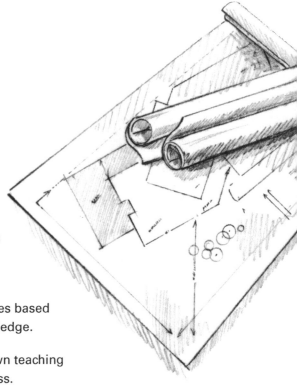

# Reflection and Action

▶ How do you get feedback about your teaching behaviors?

▶ Which behaviors resonated with you?

▶ What challenged your thinking? What did you agree with? What did you disagree with?

▶ Reflect on the HIT 25 list. Make an effort to increase your ratio of high-impact behaviors.

# In the Library

### Teaching Behaviors

*Power of Teaching—The Science of the Art: Behavioral Pathway to Teaching Excellence* (2009)
Dr. Joseph Wise, David Sundstrom

*"Teaching Skillful Teaching" Educational Leadership* (December 2010/January 2011 Vol. 68, #4, p. 40–45)
Deborah Loewenberg Ball, Francesca Forzani

### Classroom Management

*The First Days of School: How to Be an Effective Teacher* (2004)
Harry K. Wong, Rosemary T. Wong

*CHAMPS, 2nd Edition: A Proactive and Positive Approach to Classroom Management* (1998)
Randall S. Sprick, Ph.D.

# Journal Entry

**Experiencing and Personalizing your Journey**

**Academy Awards:** Although not many people like seeing themselves on camera, at this point in your journey consider having a colleague film an upcoming lesson. Flip cameras are an easy and affordable way to do this.

Once the lesson is over, load the digital content on your computer. Watch the lesson by yourself. That's right—by yourself. No one else needs to see it. Document here what you said and did. What your students said. How do your behaviors compare to the effective teaching behaviors in this chapter?

The first time I saw myself teach on camera I was mortified! It is a natural feeling. Once you get past noticing all of your quirks, focus in on your teaching behaviors. It will be a powerful experience.

**What I Did:**

**What I Said:**

**What My Students Said:**

# Managing
## Student Performance

From multiple sources, collect and analyze evidence of student learning to understand each student's mastery of specific content and readiness for new content.

After planning for and teaching our classroom blueprint, we introduce Core Principle 4, Managing Student Performance. A highly-effective teacher reflects upon their teaching and relentlessly looks for ways to increase effectiveness. In doing so, their classroom blueprint becomes a living document that is monitored and adjusted based upon timely and relevant information. Our journey draws to a close by considering three questions:

1. What information do I use to reflect upon my teaching?

2. How often do I do this?

3. How should I do this?

Chapter 10—Collaborate and Analyze Results: Teacher Teams Accelerate Performance demonstrates how you and your colleagues can build a supportive and creative network to help build change into your teaching and your students' learning and performance. A common goal, language, calendars, and data will become your collaborative allies.

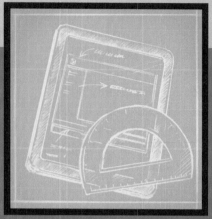

## Core Principle 1
### Designing with Purpose

Design a blueprint for classroom instruction and strategically consider a range of choices to motivate student success.

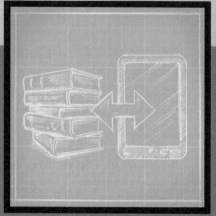

## Core Principle 2
### Customizing 21st Century Learning

Know the 21st century learner, leverage a range of advanced technology tools that will provide multiple learning pathways that customize and enrich the learning experience.

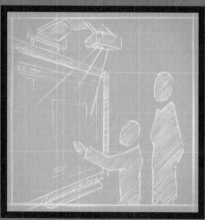

## Core Principle 3
### High-Impact Teaching Behaviors

Teach the blueprint by using a series of high-impact behaviors associated with student learning.

## Core Principle 4
### Managing Student Performance

From multiple sources, collect and analyze evidence of student learning to understand each student's mastery of specific content and readiness for new content.

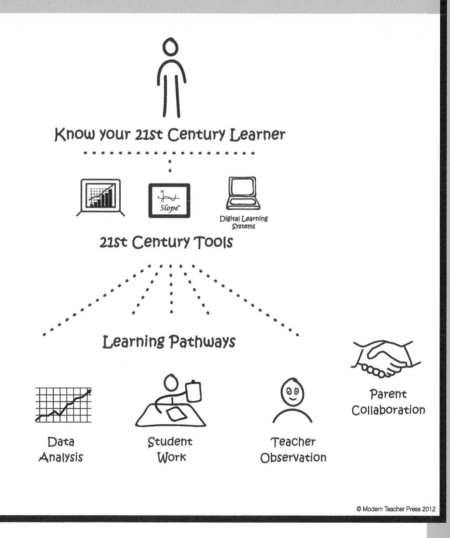

## Managing Student Performance

Know your 21st Century Learner

Slope
Digital Learning Systems

21st Century Tools

Learning Pathways

Teacher Teams

Data Analysis

Student Work

Teacher Observation

Parent Collaboration

© Modern Teacher Press 2012

# Collaborate and Analyze Results:
## Teacher Teams Accelerate Performance

# A Teacher's Story: Good Teachers

*Edwin, a principal of an elementary school in Los Angeles, has been at the school for nearly 20 years. Beginning as a teacher's aide at that school years earlier, he was proud to be in his 5th year of the principalship.*

*From our first meeting with Edwin, we were impressed by his sincere desire to improve the lives of kids in the school's broken-down neighborhood, an area known for crime and violence. On several occasions to visit Edwin, he wasn't on site—only to learn that he was on home visits to collect students who hadn't shown up for school. Later, we'd see Edwin, clipboard in hand, walking through the front door with several children. "All from the same family," he once remarked, "That makes it 100% attendance."*

*During another visit, we asked Edwin to give us a walk-through of several classrooms. We often ask principals to describe their observations of the instruction. On this morning, we visited a third grade teacher's classroom for about 20 minutes. On our way to the next classroom, Edwin said, "Ya, she's a good teacher." When we asked what he meant by good teacher he responded, "She teaches well. The kids really like her. But she's tough." We asked, "What do you mean by teaches well?" He was stuck for words. He was certain of her effectiveness, but—put on the spot—couldn't articulate why. When we followed up later, student achievement data revealed that the vast majority of her students were making **over a year's worth of academic growth,** far outpacing other classrooms across the city. Edwin was correct, and had a sincere desire to communicate how effective he believed her to be, but didn't have the language to do so.*

## Collaboration, Protocols and Data

This chapter begins by helping you think about collaboration. It generates ideas for you and your colleagues to get precise with the language you use and offers educational protocols for communicating about data, one part of designing successful classrooms. Finally, by reviewing quantitative data on student performance coupled with analysis of student work and qualitative information, this chapter frames how to manage the learning in your classroom.

# Connect and Reflect

In our work with teachers, principals, and schools around the country, we found a general inability to communicate about teaching. The language of our profession varies from school to school and among classrooms, making it difficult to talk about our practice with specificity. As I was traveling oversees last year, I was struck by how other industries not only have a common language, but protocols that aid in formal communication about their practice.

It was 4:00 pm and I was sitting in the Luang Prabang, Laos International Airport waiting for a flight to Hanoi, Vietnam. There were only a few seats, one gate, and travelers had to walk onto the runway to board the plane. As I thought about my flight, I was struck by the flight industry's granular language and descriptions of tactical moves when taking off or landing. Would there be any reason to doubt that the pilot of my flight would veer from the profession's tactical moves and decide to fly the plane using his own style? According to the 2005 New Normal Checklist, I should be confident that, before my flight to Hanoi, the pilot will perform the following:

| | | |
|---|---|---|
| **Preflight** | Oxygen | Tested, 100% |
| | NAVIGATION Transfer and DISPLAY Switches | NORMAL, AUTO |
| | Window Heat | On |
| | Pressurization Mode Selector | AUTO |
| | Flight Instruments | Heading___ Altimeter___ |
| | Parking Brake | Set |
| | Engine Start Levers | CUTOFF |
| **Before Taxi** | Generators | ON |
| | Probe Heat | ON |
| | Anti-Ice | _____ |
| | Engine Start Switches | CONT |
| | Auto brake | RTO |
| | Flight controls | Checked |
| | Ground equipment | Clear |
| **Before Takeoff** | Flaps | Green light |
| | Stabilizer trim | ___ Units |

As a passenger, are you anxious or reassured by these standards and protocols? The flight industry has created a language to communicate specific information regarding different elements of their work as well as precision with order. In doing so, they have aligned the language to a number of grain-size moves that articulate standards in the profession about what pilots are supposed to do. This has led to increased safety for passengers.

## A New Normal for the Teaching Profession

Many professions have successful collaborative lexicons, and skilled practitioners adapt within different contexts. It is time for, like the airline industry, the teaching profession to develop a "new normal" —a shared lexicon that allows us to confidently communicate within our own school, with others in our community, and across state borders.

Have you found yourself struggling to describe various aspects of teaching? Do you communicate easily with other teachers about your practice? How do you communicate with other teachers about our work? How often? I am sure you have also experienced the different ways—and words—our profession uses to communicate about teaching. Most recently, we were in a conversation with three other teachers when we realized that all were using a different definition of the word *curriculum*. We hope you will become inspired and empowered to start developing a common language at your school.

Educators need a common language to be able to discuss, with specificity, aspects of our practice (instruction) and content (curriculum). We have seen the power behind teachers communicating about teaching with each other using specific, precise, descriptive language. Work to create a common professional language at your own school.

### Developing Your Common Language: A Glossary

The airline industry's precision in language increased safety because the common operating language is consistent whether flying to Santa Fe or Shanghai. We can learn from this example.

First, take the time to generate a list of words associated with everyday teaching practices. Your list might include words like the following.

Instructional Materials • Assessment • Textbook
Pedagogy • Publisher • Flexible Grouping • Curriculum
Differentiation • Scaffolding • Independent Reading
Guided Reading • Shared Reading • Read-Alouds

Second, have a conversation about what each of your words mean. Co-create a Glossary of Terms your school will use to communicate about practice. This glossary could be titled: *"What We Mean at Betsy Ross Elementary When We Say…"* Add to and modify this list throughout the year. This list could also be used in new teacher trainings at your school or district to help new teachers become better acquainted with the school and its professional practice.

Next, create a shared understanding of precise language around content. Important differences are often hidden beneath broad, general content standards. For instance, "Ratios and Proportional Relationships," is a group of new Common Core Content Standards organized into *domains;* this domain is specific to 6th–7th grade mathematics and encompasses several Grade-Level Specific Standards involving content from ratios and proportions. Would everyone on your grade level team understand precisely what content you were referring to if you used this language?

Getting specific about content language is a necessary ingredient in data analysis. If teachers leave a Teacher Team Meeting after having diagnosed root causes for why students in the 6th grade performed poorly on ratios on the last assessment, but have different understandings of the content needed to re-teach to students, even a customized learning plan won't yield improved performance on ratios on the next assessment. Get absolutely clear at the front end of teacher team meetings about what colleagues mean when they are talking about content. It's initially awkward and slows things down, but you will develop a shared understanding of content language before beginning analysis collaboration.

# Why We Do What We Do

Establishing routines around collaboration and performance is one of the most important levers teachers have for improving their practice. While this book is written for the individual classroom teacher as the main audience, leveraging teacher collaboration is critical.

## Establish a Cadence of Collaboration and Performance

In our work with thousands of teachers in hundreds of schools across the country, we have discovered that those who accelerate the pace of results do it by establishing a collaborative and performance-driven culture. No one can do it alone. The idea is progress, not perfection. Highly-effective teachers continuously seek to improve their results and understand this is a journey, not a destination.

## Protocols and Data Analysis

When teams get together, with the right data, there should be a structured approach—a protocol— to communicating and a method to **asking good questions** (good questions are really quite simple). Protocols are practical and useful tools for collaborative teams to analyze data. A good educational assessment protocol is designed to understand *why* a student is not learning and to get at the root of it.

One very helpful reference is Joseph McDonald's *The Power of Protocols: An Educator's Guide to Better Practice*. McDonald and his colleagues detail over 20 protocols that teachers and school administrators can use to structure teacher team meetings, ILT meetings, or other meetings that involve analyzing data or student work.

Every meeting does not need a protocol. While protocols can be helpful by keeping conversations focused and tight, they aren't the only approach. However, without the structure they provide, make sure your team moves beyond surface analysis of the data or student work and digs deeper into *why* students are experiencing misconceptions about material. We have witnessed teacher teams creating their own powerful protocols to get at root cause analysis.

## Teacher Teams

Weekly teacher team collaboration begins with a specific purpose: work together for planning, instruction, and analysis of student achievement. In many cases, teacher teams, grade-level teams, or departments are already in place, but be careful that the content of conversations has an instructional focus. Conversations can often drift towards scheduling, weekly logistics, upcoming field trips, or parent complaints. Establish clear expectations about an instructional focus.

Weekly collaboration should focus in on a few key topics.

- ▶ Set goals
- ▶ Weekly lesson planning
- ▶ Intentional pedagogical choices
- ▶ Specific instructional strategies
- ▶ Standards alignment
- ▶ Review of student work
- ▶ Analysis of informal checks for understanding and formal assessments

Longer and more intensive teacher teaming is also useful. In one particular district, teachers collaborated in *End of Instructional Cycle Teacher Team Meetings.* These collaboration meetings were aligned to the established instructional cycles that you read about in *Designing with Purpose.* These meetings were longer, usually from 3 to 5 hours, and focused in on a few key topics.

## End of Instructional Cycle Teacher Team Meeting Goals:

A thorough analysis of the end-of-unit assessments

▶ A reflection of the instructional strategies used during the unit

▶ A student-by-student, name-by-name review of who mastered what standards

▶ Action plans to re-teach content and standards not yet mastered

▶ A preview of the next unit's assessments

▶ Backwards mapping the next 4 to 6 weeks of instruction with the end-of-unit goals in mind

▶ Scaffolding plans for the skills needed to be end-of-unit successful

▶ Identifying the big ideas of the unit and a plan to connect the numerous discrete skills into a larger idea or theme

▶ Key instructional strategies that will be used

Whether meeting briefly for weekly collaboration or for longer sessions at the end of instructional cycles, collaborative teacher teams are effective because their work is all about improving teacher practice and student achievement. There is a tight alignment between how students are doing in class and how (and how often) their teachers are continuously monitoring and adjusting their instruction. This integrated approach—between results, teacher practice, and teacher collaboration, accelerated the pace of student performance and success.

## Instructional Leadership Teams (ILTs)

Instructional Leadership Teams (ILTs) are another vehicle for teacher and administrator collaboration. While Teacher Teams focus primarily on grade level and individual classroom analysis, the unit of analysis for instructional leadership teams is the school itself. At their core, ILTs are responsible for the organizational learning in the school. Strong instructional leadership teams help define if the school is indeed a *learning organization.*

> *Instructional leadership teams understand their primary function: create and acquire new knowledge based upon data and then transfer that knowledge by modifying organizational behavior into concrete actionable plans.*

## Becoming a "Learning Organization"

David Garvin, in "Building a Learning Organization," defines a learning organization as one, "Skilled at creating, acquiring, and transferring knowledge, and at modifying its behavior to reflect new knowledge and insights" (pg. 80). Instructional leadership teams meet usually once or twice per month in meetings that are scheduled before the start of the school year and reflected on the school's instructional calendar. The meetings always begin with a set agenda which accurately reflects the most recent and timely data available.

## Turn Data into Norms and Action

To function effectively, ILTs need to have a strong process for data analysis that is focused on the skills and sub-skills students need to master. Key takeaways are translated into teacher action, and teacher action is always aligned to standards (as you read Chapters 1 and 3). Meetings often have a structured protocol and agenda to help the process.

Establishing norms helps build trust through this process. While every adult in the school should feel a sense of ownership for student learning, teachers need time to strengthen their craft. Spend time on the front-end setting norms for how these conversations will take place and revisit the norms frequently. The key is to develop teachers' analytical skills. Depersonalizing the data helps foster collaborative inquiry about the assessment results and accelerates a shared and actionable instructional solution.

Structures like the ones described above craft the culture of organizations. Like a heartbeat, you can feel the rhythm of it—and it becomes the pulse of the organization, school, department, or grade-level team. And like a heartbeat, if it stops, the system starts to shut down. Many teachers already serve on school leadership teams, so while the idea is not new, focusing on results, analysis, and action improves the concept. Remember to celebrate progress along the way.

## Adding to your Instructional Calendar

As you read in Chapter 4, creating an instructional calendar begins by plotting the dates you will assess your students. School, district, or state-mandated assessments are usually scheduled well in advance, but it is typical for classroom-generated assessments that occur more frequently to evolve with the pacing of instruction. Regardless, begin the school year with all of the mandated assessments documented on your instructional calendar and a general idea of when end-of-unit assessments will occur. Daily and weekly assessments, often more informal, will make the instructional calendar a living document.

We have found in our work with teachers that schools that plan their collaborative routines around the scheduled assessments on the front end find it easier to implement and stick with it.

Schools have many opportunities to leverage instructionally-focused time, and Teacher Teams and Instructional Leadership Teams are a great beginning opportunity for teachers and administrators to collaborate. Identify the times you and your colleagues can collaborate about student performance. Now, add these dates to the Instructional Calendar you created in Chapter 4. Check to see if collaboration times coincide with assessment results. There should be a natural rhythm and pattern to the instructional calendar. Collaboration and assessment go hand-in-hand.

# Guiding Questions

▶ After reading the airplane story, what are you left thinking about?

▶ What benefits would come from a common language?

▶ What benefits would come from structured collaboration and teaming?

▶ What roadblocks are there to this type of work?

▶ Why is collaboration important for our work as teachers?

▶ How do you think about results and student performance? Who is responsible for it?

# Connecting to Classroom Practice

## Assessment Analysis: Individual and Team

Individual teachers think about and informally analyze assessment results daily. Your informal checks for understanding and teacher observations— and your analysis of this information—are powerful practices. On a more formal and scheduled basis, teachers collaboratively analyze student performance. As you read, teacher teams and instructional leadership teams assist teachers in making informed decisions on how best to adjust their instructional plans.

As the team uncovers potential root causes for performance, plan time to **re-teach**. Document in your unit and lesson plans when you will re-teach, how you will do it, and which students can be helped. Include multiple strategies to customize student learning. Finally, always document who is responsible for the **follow-up**.

*When teachers formally analyze assessment results it helps convey what works in concrete ways. Data documents and identifies the instructional practices that help students master content in meaningful ways; conversely, it helps identify which choices did not work.*

## Begin With the Data: Analytics Increases Effectiveness

The process always begins with **data**—with *what you know*. Each of these collaborative teams must have the right data. Data can come in many forms and includes student work, end-of-unit assessments, informal classroom assessments, state or national assessments, student conferences, or teacher observations. However, for it to be of most value, data needs to be timely and relevant. Use this data to generate a story, for this particular moment in time, about what is happening with one student, groups of students, a classroom, a grade level, a school, or a district. The data should also be a measure of what you intend to measure—the standards and skills you want your students to learn.

As the team uncovers some potential root causes for performance, you will want to create **customized learning plans.** You are already familiar with many different strategies to customize student learning from data. Finally, document who is responsible for the **follow-up.**

## Absolute and Selected Response

If your team is analyzing selected response assessments, begin with **item analysis,** which will help you to understand several things.

> ▶ A global perspective on how most of the class did relative to learning the outcomes

> ▶ A deep-dive perspective to understand kid-by-kid, name-by-name mastery of specific skills and standards

> ▶ A reflection of test design and the skills students needed to answer the questions

> ▶ Student engagement

> ▶ A reflection of the alignment of curriculum, instruction and assessment: Did I teach what was assessed?

> ▶ The instructional strategies used during the unit and if they were the most effective

The teacher's ability to know and respond to student misunderstanding of content is one of the most powerful elements of instruction. Evidence of student learning includes listening to a student's oral responses during a lesson, examining authentic student work, and selected and constructed response. **Distracter analysis** is a built-in tool for teachers to use on some selected response assessments. If you are creating your own assessments, it can be difficult to build in this tool; in some cases, districts will design selected response assessments with this in mind.

*Over a 12-month period, we were privy to the implementation of a structured approach to collaboration **at every level** of a particular school system. Part of the success was because very clear expectations about the frequency of collaboration were laid out for teachers and administrators.*

## Evidence that Routines Build Culture

Routines are important at every level of the system. For instance, in our most recent work with schools we observed, and in some cases led, establishing routines for weekly and monthly collaborative conversations. As we participated, we observed that talking about the current reality of student performance is sometimes difficult, confusing, and uncomfortable. But, as we've also witnessed, schools and organizations that bravely confront the reality of student performance and act to develop a cadence of collaboration more often than not *accelerate* their performance.

Establishing a cadence of collaboration begins to shift schools into a performance-driven culture. We fully recognize this may not be within the span of control for one classroom teacher. However, a classroom teacher may have influence over his or her grade level team and could start there.

### The Analysis

To begin the analysis, you will need what we call the *Critical Five*:

1. The assessment

2. The report or student work

3. A protocol for data analysis (not necessary but helpful)

4. A copy of the standards

5. Customized Learning Plan (see Chapter 8)

Next step is to understand the report and all of the information contained in it, including how the data is reported and what it means. One of the most helpful resources for data analysis is *Driven by Data* (2010) by Paul Bambrick-Santoyo. This book includes numerous examples for improving analysis skills and transcends state-to-state differences within assessments.

This chapter is all about collaboration and continuous improvement. Embed these analyses and reflection practices into your daily, weekly, and monthly routines.

## Blueprint Essentials

Use data to form a continuous improvement cycle using your classroom blueprint.

Continuously monitor and adjust your blueprint based upon timely and relevant information.

Build routines and procedures for analyzing student performance. Routines and procedures create a culture of improvement and success.

Leverage 21st century technology tools to accelerate student pacing of content or slow it down. This will help customize your classroom instruction based upon individual students' academic readiness factors. Assigning instructional playlists can be an effective way to respond to your analysis of data.

# Reflection and Action

## Reflection

▶ How often to you analyze assessment results?
Do you include student work?

▶ Do you collaborate with colleagues when you do this?

▶ Do you find collaboration helpful? Why or why not?

▶ Would you and your colleagues benefit from
a common language?

## In the Library

### Protocols

*The Power of Protocols: An Educator's
Guide to Better Practice, 2nd Edition* (2007)
Joseph McDonald, Nancy Mohr, Alan Dichter

### Data Analysis

*Data Wise: A Step by Step Guide to Using Assessment
Results to Improve Teaching and Learning* (2005)
Parker, City, and Murnane

*Driven by Data* (2010)
Paul Bambrick-Santoyo

# Journal Entry

**Experiencing and
Personalizing your Journey**

**Teacher Architect Date**: It is time to schedule another teacher architect date. This time, take an hour or two out of your week to visit a local gallery or museum. Find an exhibit that piques your interest. What is the artist trying to communicate? How do you think the artist re-imagined their medium to create this exhibit?

You are probably wondering what this has to do with data. Possibly nothing. But, it is important in your journey to do things you don't always do—and different kinds of experiences have the potential to unlock new thinking.

**Blank Canvas**: Create your own artwork here—and it doesn't have to have anything to do with teaching. It's your canvas!

# Closing and Call to Action

## Teaching matters most.

It seems ordinary until you consider the scope of it: over the course of a day, week, month, and school year, you alone make thousands of decisions, both deliberate and instinctive, that affect how your students think and what they will learn. What we have discovered is that it is quite complex– *a complexity that deserves attention, support, and empowerment.*

You are the architect of learning, designing both physical and virtual spaces for your students to flourish. You became the instructional architect the moment you began to make intentional choices in your planning and teaching. You have been called upon, each for your own reason, to respond to our society's new **ask.** This new ask calls upon our nation's teachers to rethink and reimagine 21st century classrooms; classrooms that encourage creativity and collaboration, social and academic networking, intellectually curious learners, and experiences that are authentic to digital natives.

We have written this book to help connect isolated parts of planning and teaching, seeking to put them together into a coherent whole. When the parts come together it can feel overwhelming and we don't want to shy away from that. Teaching *for* 21st century learning is complex, messy, nuanced, detailed, and intentional. The greatest gift we as teachers have is our ability to make choices, each and every day, some small and others quite large, that **deeply** affect the learning experience for students. Our job is to cultivate that gift by finding ways to strengthen our craft, collaborate with colleagues, and deepen our professional knowledge.

We hope you have enjoyed taking this journey with us. More importantly though, we hope this journey has empowered you with information to design a classroom blueprint to the specifications of the 21st century. Remember, it is a journey—commit to the process and find support and strength within the education community.

Our time is now. Our challenge is clear. Our instructional choices are before us. Your classroom blueprint has the power and potential to shape the next generation of Americans. Onward forward.

## About the Authors

### Shawn K. Smith

Dr. Shawn K. Smith is currently serving as a founding partner and President of Modern Teacher, an educational media and technology company focused on maximizing teaching effectiveness. Born and raised in the Midwest, Shawn is a former elementary and middle school teacher, assistant principal, principal, director of curriculum, instruction, and assessment, and most recently Chief of Schools for the nation's third largest school system, Chicago Public Schools. For the past 15 years Shawn has served inside four different public education school systems in California and Illinois. He has also taught as an adjunct professor for several universities.

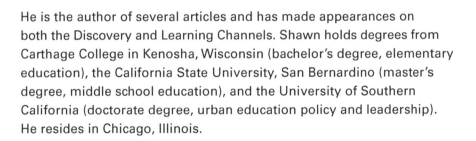

He is the author of several articles and has made appearances on both the Discovery and Learning Channels. Shawn holds degrees from Carthage College in Kenosha, Wisconsin (bachelor's degree, elementary education), the California State University, San Bernardino (master's degree, middle school education), and the University of Southern California (doctorate degree, urban education policy and leadership). He resides in Chicago, Illinois.

## Ann M. Chavez

Dr. Ann M. Chavez is currently serving as a founding partner and Chief Academic Officer of ModernTeacher, an educational media and technology company focused on maximizing teaching effectiveness and deeply committed to supporting teachers. She is a native Southern Californian and currently resides in Henderson, Nevada. Ann has 24 years of experience across all levels of public school service. As a teacher and principal, she worked in school districts across Southern California. As a district leader, she most recently served in Chicago Public

Schools as the Deputy of Curriculum, Instruction, and Assessment for a regional area on Chicago's Southside. Ann believes that we find the path to results by providing focused support for teachers and empowering principals as instructional leaders. Ann uses a practical hands-on approach and brings her daily experience as both teacher and principal as she mentors and coaches today's educational leaders. She focuses on the individual needs of districts and school sites to build the leadership capacity within and empowers them to make strategic decisions that directly affect student learning outcomes.

Ann earned a Bachelor's degree in Liberal Studies from California State University of Long Beach, a Masters of Education in School Administration from Azusa Pacific University, and a Doctorate of Education in Educational Leadership in Urban Schools K–12 from the University of Southern California.

Ann enjoys traveling around the country meeting and working with educators; she also loves to travel for relaxation, exploration, and personal growth. She enjoys being outdoors, going for a long run, loves to cook, and cherishes spending time with family, friends, and her four-legged buddies Missy, Max, and Rosie.

## Garrett W. Seaman

Garrett Seaman has spent the past eight years as a teacher and school district administrator, studying and perfecting instructional strategies around effectively integrating technology and media. He is currently serving as a founding partner and Director of Educational Operations for Modern Teacher. In addition to training students, teachers, and administrators on how to best capitalize on the participatory-web, Garrett is versed in: website development, instructional software, educational assessments, and is an expert in understanding how the learner interacts with multiple technologies. Garrett's ongoing mission has been to *continuously re-define effective instructional technology in the modern classroom.*

Garrett earned his B.A. from the University of Illinois, M.A. from Aurora University and is currently conducting research at Northern Illinois University on how the role of the instructional technologist effectively functions in urban school systems. With the completion of this research he hopes to apply this knowledge to both private and public sector technology leadership roles.

Garrett lives outside of Chicago in Lombard, Illinois, with his wife Kimberly and son Everett, and has a personal passion for tech. He is inspired knowing that *technology transcends all ages and all applications* and believes that anyone can utilize technology to solve problems and make experiences richer.

# Acknowledgements

## Our Collective Thanks

We consider it a privilege to serve America's public schools and for over two decades the three of us have done just that. We have learned so much from the people we have worked with and this book is a collection of the combined knowledge we've gained through the years. One of the greatest joys about being a teacher comes from the countless things you learn from your students. Throughout this project we have tried to keep student learning as the purpose of this work. Our collective thanks to all of the people we have worked with and to all of the students we have taught; the lessons we have learned from you have shaped Teacher as Architect.

To our editor, Andrea Swank—thank you for taking a trio of rookie writers and guiding us through a year-long project that became a labor of love for all of us. Your patience, support, guidance, and encouragement provided a roadmap for us to complete this work. Thank you for believing in this project and encouraging us to take risks. You repeatedly worked to bring balance and clarity to our writing, by editing and organizing our words into a coherent manuscript. This could not have been possible without your collaboration. Thank you.

This book was also greatly enhanced by the creative energy, contributions, feedback, and support from a handful of colleagues. First, our sincere gratitude and thanks goes out to Dr. Amy Zaher. Her feedback throughout the writing of this manuscript was invaluable. Her attention to detail, knowledge of educational research, and professional experience helped shape this project.

We are also indebted to Nicholas Gaines for his contributions and expertise regarding classroom culture and student behavior. His insights into effective teaching behaviors provided many useful examples for this manuscript. He is a true instructional leader.

Four additional colleagues, Dr. Stuart Gothold, Dr. Mike Walls, Dr. Irvin Howard, and Dr. Joseph Wise also deserve special thanks. We have so much respect for the work they have accomplished in public education. We consider all of these gentlemen mentors, colleagues, and friends. Thank you.

This project was also greatly enhanced by the creative direction of Bob Tulini. His attention to detail and his ability to manage both us and our creative contributors proved to be a cherished resource. Thank you.

A final thank you to our visual team beginning first with our amazing graphic designers, Ed, Sandi and Lisa, for bringing function and aesthetics into perfect balance. And a special thanks to Jeanine Hattas, and Shawn-Erik Toth—both of whom also helped bring this book visually to life.

# Our Personal Thanks

### Shawn

There are many people who personally supported me through this entire project. My greatest thanks are reserved for my partner, Dr. Richard Ezgur, who for an entire year had to hear my daily updates—truly taking on this journey with me. Your emotional support and encouragement combined with your chiropractic support proved to be the perfect remedy for a first time writer! All my love. Thank you to my parents, Kevin and Cathy, for believing in my ability to write a book and for continuous support and encouragement throughout the writing process. Thank you to my sister Shannon and her husband Chad, who were a continuous source of positive feedback. May this book inspire Taylor, Easton, and Nate's teachers to design 21st century instruction. Thanks to my brother, Cory, who kept everything in perspective for me, reminding me of life beyond this work. Special thanks to my extended family the Ezgurs: Harlie, Jerry, Wendi, Michael, Aidan, Charlie and Rosie for your kind words of encouragement and support. An additional thanks to Wendi Ezgur for your continuous flow of energy, creativity, and ideas! Your supply is endless!

### Ann

I begin with a heartfelt thank you to my parents, Andy and Pam, who have always loved, encouraged and supported me in all my endeavors, including this one. A big hug and thumbs up to my brother, Chris, who always keeps me smiling and reminds me to enjoy the little things in life each day. Love and thanks to my Aunt Kathy for her unconditional, "I'll do anything," support—especially over this last year. Cheers to Jacki and Margaret, mi amigas, for the endless love, laughs, and encouragement no matter what life brings. This year and this project could not have happened without your support! To my friend and colleague, Amy, much love and appreciation for the quality educator and person that you are—your encouragement and collaboration on this book and in life mean so much to me. A special thanks to Susan and Don, inspiring teachers and colleagues whose wisdom and guidance along the way have been an enduring influence that have shaped and guided me into the educator I am today. And a special thanks to Professor Gothold, your spirit and dedication to improving education for all students will always inspire me to do my best to serve our children. Fight on!

## Garrett

Above all, I would like to thank my wife Kimberly for giving me the strength and motivation throughout this project. In addition to her continuous personal support, Kim's professional teaching expertise has made my contributions to this book more instructionally sound and thoughtful. During this work we were blessed with our firstborn, Everett, who I hope will be personally inspired by educators driven to be the "Modern Teacher" in their 21st century instructional design and delivery. Thank you to my parents, Craig and Dianne, who have provided me with a lifetime of encouragement and the means to be the best educator I can be. Thank you to my Grandma Maureen and my late Grandfather Everett, who through many of his own thoughtful discussions drove me to stay sharp and continue to hone my skills. Thank you to my Sister Tracy and family, Joel, Katherine and Ryan for always supporting me and keeping me in your thoughts. Finally, thank you to my extended parents, Russ and Julie, your encouragement and business-minded advice have provided a perfect balance to this endeavor.

# References

www.acheivethecore.org, (2012)

Anderson, L., Evertson, C., & Brophy, J., *An experimental study of effective teaching in first grade reading groups,* (1979), The Elementary School Journal, 79

Anderson, Lorin W., et al. (David R. Krathwohl, Peter W. Airasian, Kathleen A. Cruikshank, Richard E. Mayer, Paul R. Pintrich, James Raths, Merlin C. Wittrock), *A Taxonomy for Learning, Teaching and Assessing: A Revision of Bloom's Taxonomy of Educational Objectives* (2001)

Bambrick-Santoyo, Paul, *Driven by Data*, (2010)

Banchi, H., Bell, R., "The Many Levels of Inquiry" *Science and Children,* (October 2008)

Bandura, Albert, Walters, R., *Social Learning and Personality Development* (1963)

Bandura, Albert, *Social Learning Theory* (1976)

Beers, Sue, *Teaching 21st Century Skills*, (2011)

Bell, Randy, *The Many Levels of Inquiry* (2008)

Berk, L. Berk, Winsler, A., "Vygotsky: His Life and Works" and "Vygotsky's Approach to Development," *Scaffolding Children's Learning: Vygotsky and Early Childhood Learning.* National Association for Education of Young Children (1995)

Bergmann, J., Sams, A., *Flipped Classroom* (2012)

Bloom, Benjamin, et al., *A Taxonomy of Educational Goals and Objectives: Handbook I: Cognitive Domain* (1956)

Bloom et al., *A Taxonomy of Educational Objectives: Affective Domain Handbook II* (1964)

Brooks and Brooks, *In Search of Understanding: The Case for Constructivist Classrooms* (1993)

Brunn, Peter, *The Lesson Plan Handbook: Essential Strategies that Inspire Student Thinking and Learning* (2010)

Cajori, Florian, *The Teaching and History of Mathematics in the United States, Public Domain Document* (Pgs 45–52)

Cash, Richard M., *Advancing Differentiation, Thinking and Learning for the 21st Century* (2011)

Christensen, Clayton, Johnson, Curtis W., Horn, Michael B., *Disrupting Class: How Disruptive Innovation Will Change the Way the World Learns* (2008)

Common Core State Standards Initiative (February 22, 2011) Common Core State Standards Initiative website: http://www.corestandards.org

http://www.curriculummapping101.com

http://www.curriculum21.com

Darch, C., & Carnine, D, *Teaching content area material to learning disabled students*. Exceptional Children, (1986)

Dell'Olio, J., Donk, T., *Models of Teaching: Connecting Student Learning with Standards*, (2007) p. 346–348

Dochy, F., Alexander, P., "Mapping prior knowledge: A framework of discussion among researchers" (1995) *European Journal of Psychology in Education, 10,* 224–242

Driscoll, M. P., *Psychology of learning for instruction* (2005)

Dweck, Carol, *Mindset* (2006)

Dweck, C.S., and Molden, D.C., "Self-theories: Their impact on competence motivation and acquisition" (2005), *Handbook of competence and motivation*

Eggen, Paul, Kauchak, Don P., *Educational Psychology: Windows on Classrooms, 8th edition* (1997)

Florida, Richard, *The Rise of the Creative Class: And How It's Transforming Work, Leisure, Community, and Everyday Life* (2003)

Florida, Richard, *Who's Your City? How the Creative Economy Is Making Where to Live the Most Important Decision of Your Life* (2008)

*Frascati Manual: Proposed Standard of Practice for Surveys on Research and Experimental Development*, 6th edition, Organisation for Economic Co-operation and Development (OECD), p.69. (2002)

Friedman, Thomas L., *Hot, Flat, and Crowded: Why We Need a Green Revolution—and How It Can Renew America* (2008)

Friedman, Thomas L., *The World Is Flat: A Brief History of the Twenty-first Century* (2005)

Gagne, Robert M., Driscoll, M., *Essentials of Learning for Instruction* (1988)

Gagne, Robert M., *Conditions of Learning* (1977)

Gardner, Howard, *Five Minds for the Future* (2007)

Gardner, Howard, *Frames Of Mind: The Theory of Multiple Intelligences* (1983)

Gardner, Howard, *Truth, Beauty, and Goodness Reframed: Educating for the Virtues in the Twenty-First Century* (2012)

Gavin, David, "Building a Learning Organization" *Harvard Business Review* (July-August 1993)

Goldberg, Mark F., *Lessons from Exceptional School Leaders* (2001)

Hale, Janet, *A Guide to Curriculum Mapping: Planning, Implementing, and Sustaining the Process* (2009)

Hammerman, Elizabeth, *Eight Essentials for Inquiry-Based Science,* (2005)

Horn and Staker, *The Rise of K–12 Blended Learning* (2011)

Hunter, Madeline Hunter, *Mastery Teaching: Increasing Instructional Effectiveness in Elementary and Secondary Schools, Colleges, and Universities* (1982)

Jacobs, Heidi Hayes, *Mapping the Big Picture: Integrating Curriculum and Assessment, K–12* (1997)

Jacobs, Heidi Hayes, *The Curriculum Mapping Planner: Templates, Tools and Resources for Effective Professional Development* (2004)

Jacobs, Heidi Hayes, *Curriculum 21: Essential Education for a Changing World* (2010)

Jacobs, Heidi Hayes, ASCD, *Curriculum 21: Essential Education for a Changing World* (2010)

Januszeqski, A., Molenda M., *Educational technology: A definition with commentary* (2008) Association for Educational Communical Technology (Eds.) pgs. 1–14

Kearsley, G., Shneiderman, B, "Engagement Theory: A Framework for Technology-Based Teaching and Learning" (1998) *Educational* Technology, Vol. 38, No. 5, pgs. 20–23 (1998)

Kendall, John, *Understanding Common Core Standards* (2011)

Krawthwohl, David, *A Taxonomy of Educational Objectives, The Classification of Educational Goals: Affective Domain Handbook II* (1964)

Lemov, Doug, *Teach Like a Champion: 49 Techniques that Put Students on the Path to College* (2010)

Levine, Mel, *A Mind at a Time,* (2002)

Loewenberg Ball, D. Forzani F., "Teaching Skillful Teaching" (December 2010/January 2011), *Educational Leadership,* Vol. 68, #4, p. 40–45

Mager, Robert, *Preparing Instructional Objectives* (1962)

Marzano, Robert, Kendall, John, *The New Taxonomy of Educational Objectives*, 2nd edition (2007)

Marzano, Pickering, and Pollack, *Classroom Instruction that Works* (2001)

Marzano, Robert, "What Teachers Gain from Deliberate Practice", (December 2010/January 2011), *Vol. 68, #*4 pgs. 82–85

Maslow, Abraham, *Towards a Psychology of Being* (1968)

Mcloud, Scott, Lehmann, Chris, *What School Leaders Need to Know About Digital Technologies and Social Media* (2012)

McDonald, Joseph, Mohr, Nancy, Dichter, Alan*, The Power of Protocols: An Educator's Guide to Better Practice, 2nd Edition* (2007)

Murphy, Joseph Shiffman, Catherine Dunn, *Understanding and Assessing the Charter School Movement*: *Critical Issues in Educational Leadership Series* (2002)

National Commission on Excellence in Education, *Nation at Risk: The Imperative For Educational Reform* (1983)

Paltrey, J. Palfrey, Gasser, U., Born Digital: Understanding the First Generation of Digital Natives (1999)

Parker, City, Murnane, *Data Wise: A Step by Step Guide to Using Assessment Results to Improve Teaching and Learning* (2005)

The Partnership for 21st Century Skills: http://www.21stcenturyskills.org

Partnership for the Assessment of Readiness for College and Career (PARCC): http://www.parcconline.org/

PBS *The Story of American Public Education* (February 19, 2011) Public Broadcasting System website: http://www.pbs.org/kcet/publicschool

Pink, Daniel H., *A Whole New Mind: Moving from the Information Age to the Conceptual Age* (2005)

Pulliam, J. D., Van Patten, J. J., *History of Education in America 6th Edition* (1995)

Pulliam, J. D., Van Patten, J. J., *History of Education in America 9th Edition* (2007)

Ritchhart, R., Church, M., Morrison, K., *Making Thinking Visible: How to Promote Engagement, Understanding, and Independence for All Learners.* Harvard Graduate School of Education, Project Zero (2011)

Rodgers, Carl, *Freedom to Learn* (1994)

Rothman, Robert*, Something in Common: The Common Core State Standards and the Next Chapter in American Education* (2011)

Sprick, Randall S., Ph.D., *CHAMPS, 2nd Edition: A Proactive and Positive Approach to Classroom Management* (1998)

Stiggins, Rick J., Chappuis, Jan, *Introduction to Student-Involved Assessment FOR Learning* (6th Edition) (2011)

Stiggins, Rick J., Arter, Judith A., Chappuis, Jan, Chappuis, Stephen, *Classroom Assessment for Student Learning: Doing it Right-Using it Well* (2004)

Sousa, David, *How the Brain Learns* (2001)

Tomlinson, Carol Ann, *The Differentiated Classroom: Responding to the Needs of All Learners* (1999)

Tomlinson, C. A., et. al. (2003) Differentiating Instruction in Response to Student Readiness, Interest, and Learning Profile in Academically Diverse Classrooms: A Review of Literature. Journal for the Education of the Gifted

Trilling, Bernie, Fadel, Charles, *21st Century Skills: Learning for Life in Our Times* (2009)

Udelhofen, Susan, *Keys to Curriculum Mapping: strategies and tools to make it work* (2005)

United States Department of Education (February 19, 2011) Department of Education website: http://www.ed.gov/index.html

U.S. Department of the Interior: https://www.nps.gov/jeff/william_holmes.html

Wiggens, Grant, McTighe, Jay, *Understanding by Design* (2005 Expanded 2nd edition) *The Understanding by Design Guide to Creating High Quality Units* (2011)

Wilhelm, Jeffery, *Engaging Readers and Writers with Inquiry*, (2007)

Wise, J., Sundstrom, D., *Power of Teaching—The Science of the Art: Behavioral Pathway to Teaching Excellence* (2009)

Wong, Harry K., Wong, Rosemary T., *The First Days of School: How to Be an Effective Teacher* (2004)

# Modern Teacher

An educational media company committed to supporting teachers, focused on teaching effectiveness

## We Believe

▶ in building a shared sense of purpose and meaning about our work as educators.

▶ in being reflective and continuously working on our teaching practice.

## We Are

▶ 21st century instructional design and delivery.

▶ networked for collaboration and continuous improvement.

▶ grounded in educational history and research.

▶ forward thinking.

▶ a community.

Founded in 2012, Modern Teacher is born out of the sincere desire to support teachers. We aspire to provide high-quality resources and professional development experiences for today's teachers and educational leaders.

Modern Teacher's educational media spans professional development services, publishing, online communities, collaboration events, and educational technology—all with the focus of supporting teachers and maximizing teaching effectiveness. We encourage you to explore other aspects of *ModernTeacher.com* to learn more.

# Products – TAA Signature Collection

Teacher as Architect is our signature collection from Modern Teacher Press. This collection of innovative educational tools was created and assembled to support teachers with 21st century instructional design and delivery.

*Teacher as Architect* Book

PD Kits

Cognitive Growth Targets

Instructional Alignment Tool

Questioning Flipbook

Teacher as Architect Tool Kit:

Includes the *Teacher as Architect* book, Cognitive Growth Targets, Instructional Alignment Tool, and Questioning Flip Book all in one!

## Digital Resource Library

The TAA collection is managed, stored, and accessed within the Digital Resource Library. The collection, along with additional resources, is available in a variety of digital formats and accessible on compatible mobile and tablet devices.

## Ordering Information

Visit: modernteacherpress.com/products or contact:

**Modern Teacher Press**
1-855-MTP-7776 (1-855-687-7776)
info@modernteacher.com